On The Other Side

PRENTICE-HALL INTERNATIONAL, INC., *London*
PRENTICE-HALL OF AUSTRALIA, PTY. LTD., *Sydney*
PRENTICE-HALL OF CANADA, LTD., *Toronto*
PRENTICE-HALL OF INDIA PRIVATE LTD., *New Delhi*
PRENTICE-HALL OF JAPAN, INC., *Tokyo*

KATHARINE T. HARGROVE, R.S.C.J.

Editor of the Proceedings of the
Society of Catholic College Teachers of Sacred Doctrine

On The Other Side

Prentice-Hall, Inc. *Englewood Cliffs, New Jersey*

Nihil obstat:
V. Rev. Msgr. William F. Hogan
CENSOR LIBRORUM

Imprimatur:
☒ Most Reverend Thomas A. Boland, S.T.D.
ARCHIEPISCOPUS NOVARCENCIS

Newark, New Jersey   January 18, 1967

The editor gratefully acknowledges the kind permission extended by the publishers of the following works for the use of the quotations that open the chapters of On The Other Side: Nicolas Berdyaev, *Truth and Revelation,* Harper & Brothers, copyright 1953 YMCA Press, 29 Rue St. Didier, Paris 16, France, reprinted with the permission of Harper & Row, Publishers, Inc., p. 113; Martin Buber, *I and Thou,* 2nd ed., New York, Charles Scribner's Sons, 1958, p. 101; John Dewey, *Art as Experience,* New York, G. P. Putnam's Sons, Capricorn Books, © 1958, p. 244; Paul Tillich, "Freedom and the Ultimate Concern," in John Cogley, ed., *Religion in America,* New York, Meridian Books, 1958, p. 285; Charles R. Stinnette, Jr., *Grace and the Searching of Our Heart,* New York, Association Press, 1962, p. 99; Karl Barth, *The Faith of the Church,* tr. Gabriel Vahanian, New York, Meridian Books, 1958, p. 149; Dag Hammarskjold, *Markings,* tr. Leif Sjoberg and W. H. Auden, New York, Alfred A. Knopf, © 1965, p. 112; Helmut Richard Niebuhr, *The Kingdom of God in America,* New York, Harper & Row, Publishers, Inc., 1956, p. 67; Erich Fromm, *The Heart of Man,* New York, Harper & Row, Publishers, Inc., copyright © 1964, p. 135; Robert C. Tucker, *Philosophy and Myth in Karl Marx,* Cambridge University Press, 1961, p. 223. Excerpts from the Declarations of the Ecumenical Council are taken from *The Documents of Vatican II,* published by Guild Press, America Press, and Herder and Herder, and copyrighted 1966 by America Press. Used by permission.

LIBRARY OF CONGRESS CATALOG CARD NO.: 67-16386
PRINTED IN THE UNITED STATES OF AMERICA

CURRENT PRINTING (LAST DIGIT):

10 9 8 7 6 5 4 3 2 1

Contents

On The Other Side

Traditional theology has never been the theology of the Holy Spirit.

KATHARINE T. HARGROVE, R.S.C.J.

Introduction

A word of warning is in order before you begin reading this book. Unless you take time to study the prelude to each chapter, you may find yourself going *Up the Down Staircase*. If you notice, every quotation comes from a non–Roman Catholic author. That does not mean Catholic sources were not available. Indeed, the excerpts originally chosen came from documents of Vatican II. But section 9 of the Decree on Ecumenism, stressing as it does "the importance of a more adequate understanding of the respective doctrines of our separated brethren, their history, their spiritual and liturgical life, their religious psychology and cultural background," provides the clue for the present form.

Yet if you stop where the quotation stops, you will indubitably get lost in the crowds trying to go "down the up staircase." Why? Because I deliberately quoted the authors *out of context* in order to make you do justice to them by discovering for yourself what these challenging thinkers of our day are saying to us, what demands they are making on us to examine for ourselves the complexities of our Christian experience of faith.

In the 1966 annual meeting of the Society of Catholic College Teachers of Sacred Doctrine, it became apparent to all of us that the spirit of renewal within the Church has led to an increasing awareness on the Catholic college campus of the discrepancy between the in-depth vitality of faith *qua* faith and the superficial presentation we so often give it in our teaching. Hence the sincere efforts of the speakers at that meeting to show us new means of transferring our students from the level of passive impersonalism to the level of intelligent response.

Our one regret in offering you this report of the Denver collo-

3

quium is that book length required selectivity. Each chapter bears
on some theme which has validity in its own right in the new theology. Taken in their totality, the chapters point up the principle
which unites them: the existential emphasis on the freedom of the
individual in the mature structuring of faith to choose for or against
the Church, for or against commitment to God, for or against involvement in the society of man.

Our hope is that while you are investigating *On the Other Side*
you will realize more clearly than ever that the source material available for the updating of college theology courses can be stimulating
for teachers as well as for students.

In every sphere in its own way, through each process
of becoming that is present to us,
we look out toward the fringe of the eternal Thou;
in each we are aware of a breath from the eternal Thou;
in each Thou *we address the eternal* Thou.

MARTIN BUBER

PHILIP SCHARPER

1 The Relevance of Theology to the University

When we look to the origins of our traditions in Greek civilization, we find that learning, the life of the mind, took place in a context of persons, and that the bond linking the teacher and the taught
was the bond of love, love for each other and love of truth—truth
not necessarily possessed but to be pursued. This Greek thought pattern of the life of learning is all but epitomized, for example, in the
figure of Socrates, driven by a *daemon* to make more of his fellow
citizens aware of the gulf between appearances and reality, between
that which was and that which merely seemed to be. Socrates always
lived the life of learning in the context of persons—whether he was
badgering his fellow Athenians in the market place or sitting with
his friends at a *symposium*, almost literally a drinking bout, where
the flow of good wine was nearly as constant and as heady as the
flow of good talk.

It is not the Greeks alone, however, who have contributed to that
thought pattern which places the life of learning within the context
of persons. This same thought pattern developed among the Hebrews.
Yahweh was the teacher of Israel as well as Israel's God. Hence for
the Hebrews the very understanding of the verb *to know* was predi-
cated on the fact that ideas made a difference; if they did not make
a difference, they were scarcely worth concerning oneself about. *To
know*, for the Hebrew, seemed to mean not only "to grasp concep-
tually" and to give what we would call an intellectual assent but to
experience a change from what was grasped. Unless I was changed
by what I had come to know, then I had not really come to know.
Baldly summarizing this particular Hebraic point of view, we might

say, using Newman's famous distinction, that for the Hebrews there seemed to be only real and not notional assent.

We must remind ourselves that Christ himself, the Word spoken by the God who had earlier spoken by the prophets, was also a teacher. And for him, too, Hebraic in mind, teaching took place in a highly personal context. There is thus an added poignancy in the fact that when Judas gave the sign of betrayal, he called Christ by his name as teacher: "Judas drew near to him and said to him, 'Hail, Rabbi,' and kissed him"—hail, my *teacher*, and kissed him.

Early Christianity, in trying to forge its approach to the life of the mind, drew on both Greek and Hebraic roots and combined them into a single flowering tree. Consider, for example, the rather daring experiment of Origen in founding his school at Alexandria shortly after the beginning of the third century. Having begun by setting up what we might call a catechetical institute, Origen then moved on to establish a school in the full and proper sense. The students at this school were exposed to a rather typical Greek liberal education, the education befitting a free man. But Origen pointed out to his students that this typical Greek curriculum "would be of no small help to them in the study and understanding of the Scriptures." Thus it was that Origen broke the old iron circle of humanistic studies, or at least put the old circle of humanistic studies in the context of a larger circle.

In this connection, it is interesting to recall a statement of one of Origen's pupils, Gregory of Neo-Caesarea, who studied under Origen for approximately five years:

> Nothing was forbidden us, nothing hidden from us, nothing inaccessible to us. We were to learn all manner of doctrine, barbarian or Greek, mystical or political, divine or human. We went into and examined with entire freedom all manner of ideas in order to enjoy to the full these goods of the mind. When an ancient thought was true it belonged to us and was at our disposition with all its possibilities of delightful contemplation.

The school at Alexandria represented, for its times, a search for all-inclusive knowledge, and yet it laid upon teacher and taught a more demanding task: to subsume all these truths under what the same Gregory in a memorable phrase calls "the Holy Word—the loveliest thing there is." This, I suppose, is certainly one of the things that we would mean really by a university: a *universum*, wherein the effort is made to fashion all truths into a unity. For to the Christian, in the final analysis, the word *truth*, like the word *God*, has no plural and indeed for the Christian, truth, even as God, is personal.

Moving from these origins through the span of centuries, we need but point out that this same approach to the life of the mind characterized the great Benedictine tradition which did so much to civilize Europe. If we were to strike off in a phrase the central meaning of the Benedictine tradition, we could not do better than simply cite the title of Dom LeClerq's great book on the subject, *The Love of Learning and the Desire of God*. In the Benedictine tradition, no opposition was seen between these two efforts of the human person.

Thomas Aquinas expresses perfectly this particular view of the meaning of truth and the life of learning. He insists, for example, on the unity of truth: whatever is true, regardless of who said it, is from the Holy Spirit. He reminds us that whenever we lay hold of any truth, we lay hold of the Primal Truth.

This thought pattern of the life of learning shifted in the late Middle Ages and through the Renaissance, when we see the development of a scientizing impulse which insisted upon the separation of branches of knowledge from each other and their inner ordering as integrated, autonomous disciplines. Examples of most obvious interest to our topic would be the separation of theology from philosophy and of philosophy from the physical sciences.

There is no point in arguing with the past, or of sitting doleful as we contemplate historic processes. Whether we may regret it or not (and I do not necessarily think it regrettable), this scientizing impulse would seem to have been born of the very needs of history. In any case, we see the high point of these developments in the case of René Descartes, a mathematician and philosopher who, as *philosopher*, felt it incumbent on him to roll up the past as though it were a scroll and tear it in two. He seemed to feel that all philosophy must begin again, and begin with him. After Descartes we find increasing value placed upon "the clear and distinct idea."

The life of the mind—the process of teaching and learning—became more and more removed from the context of teacher and taught linked by bonds of love with each other and with the pursuit of truth. The life of the mind now seemed to center more and more upon the absorption and the transmission of concepts. One was felt to know more of a given area of human inquiry in proportion as his mental storeroom contained a larger stock of clear, distinct ideas. At its worst, this view of the life of learning has prompted that famous definition of a university lecture as a process whereby the notes of the teacher become the notes of the student without passing through the mind of either. This thought pattern, as far as I can see, is still the model that dominates the life of learning on its higher levels in our own country. It would seem to be the grounding of the multiversity, with its attendant evils. The causes of our general student unrest are complex, of course, but it is interesting to note that one recurring cause seems to be students' reactions—either overt rebellion or smoldering resentment—to the *impersonality* of the context in which their learning takes place.

In our own time, however, we can see the development of two currents which are serving to bring about another shift, creating another thought pattern to describe and delimit the life of learning. The first of these is the notion of evolution; we have at last become aware of process. And our recovered awareness of process holds great significance for the effect it can have upon the way in which we view the life of the mind. Process reminds us that tradition, in the phrase of T. S. Eliot, is not simply a bolus to be handed on from generation to generation; properly understood, tradition is living, organic. It is a tree rather than a stone. This means that the life of the mind must now be concerned not only with "handing on a tradition" (the usual understanding of education until the beginning at least of the nineteenth century) but also with the *process of discovery*. Indeed, the students themselves are to be part of the work team contributing to the examination of tradition and even, perhaps, to the discovery of the new modes and forms in which the tradition is to realize itself.

Another major current in our time is the developing personalism which marks our stage in history. Contemporary philosophers and more lately theologians are exhibiting a concern for the person which is deeper than their predecessors have shown for centuries in our intellectual tradition. We have but to mention some names to hit off what we mean. The "I-Thou" of Buber, the stress laid by Marcel and Mounier upon "attention" and "presence" all bespeak the fact that contemporary philosophers and theologians are fingering the question of authentic humanhood. What really is a human person *au fond?*

This brief glance backward in order to look forward has, I hope, brought us to the point where we can take up the central part of our topic. I would like to discuss first the fact that the development of theology and the teaching of sacred doctrine in the Catholic college must be *ecumenical,* and under this head I would like to consider the relevance of the university to theology.

In saying that the development of theology and its teaching should mirror the Second Vatican Council by being ecumenical, we mean obviously that it must be ecumenical in the religious sense. It must go on in collaboration, shared labor, with Protestant and Jewish theology, with the other world religions and indeed with other cultures. But—to take *ecumenical* in its broadest sense—theology must also move in collaboration with the other disciplines and other areas of inquiry presented by the university. It must constantly return to the situation described by Gregory at Alexandria in 215.

If our theology were to attempt any longer to develop in isolation from other theologies, for example, then there is reason to fear that it might atrophy, because it might yield once again to the temptation to become polemical. And if theology were left to develop in isolation from other university disciplines, then it would surely fail in relevance to a marked degree and would become in effect a great frozen waterfall, with all its immense power and vitality locked and useless.

These have been broad statements, but perhaps two examples might clarify them.

First, the impact of evolution on the modern mind would seem to have had definite and deep repercussions on the development of our theology. Darwin's properly scholarly reservations about the applicability of his theories were, as you know, not heeded by others. His theories were hustled off into almost every area of human life. Had there not been a Darwin, we might ourselves have been much slower in recovering an understanding of the Church as the Mystical Body. Look, for example, at *The Catholic Encyclopedia* published in 1909 when Darwinism was still alien to most Catholic minds. Under the entry "The Mystical Body of Christ," there are about four inches of type. Monsignor Robert Hugh Benson wrote a really rather considerable book, *Christ in His Church,* in 1912. He was actually writing about the Mystical Body but seemed not to have known it, because the phrase scarcely occurs in the book itself. Further, our recovered awareness that doctrine not only does but must develop would have been much later in coming had we not been reminded of the fact of process by other disciplines.

Second, let us look at what we have called a major current of contemporary thought: personalism. This emphasis upon the person, this concern with the fundamental question of what it means really to be an authentic human being, did not originate with the theologians. Yet we see clearly the impact of the personalist orientation upon contemporary theology. Two obvious cases are the "new" personalist theology of the sacraments and the personalist theology of the act of faith, which holds that faith does not rest essentially upon giving intellectual assent to a series of propositions about God but is to be found centrally in my total and complete surrender to an invading God.

Obviously, we have not yet fully plumbed the depths of the multiple meanings of the Incarnation. To put it at its simplest: when Saint Paul said that Christ "emptied himself, taking the nature of a slave and becoming like men" (Phil. 2:7), what was he saying that would have meaning for us with the sharpness, the stabbing relevance that other statements about man have for us in our own time?

Theology alone, theology in isolation, cannot shed much more light. "Christ emptied himself, taking upon himself the form of a slave." In order to understand this facet of the Incarnation, we could use the help of the sociologist—what is the sociology of slavery? We could use the insights of a historian. We could use the commentary of an economist. We could use the revelations of a psychologist— what is a slave's psychology? Christ became, says Saint Paul, "like us in all things, sin alone excepted." Like us—but who *are* we? We have a different and, I would feel, a deeper understanding of the meaning of man than was possible for Paul. We have come to realize the layer-upon-layer that makes up our rather murky interior. The more we penetrate that interior through the insights of the depth and the developmental psychologist, the more perhaps we will realize how far and dark and deep was Christ's descent, and will begin to measure more accurately the full meaning of the "emptying of himself" of which Paul speaks.

It is important at this point to say that the collaboration between theology and other university disciplines is not necessary in order to baptize and elevate the secular disciplines. Most of these, indeed, have done and will continue to do very well, thank you, without the aid of theology. To put the matter crudely: for many behavioral scientists, social scientists, and physical scientists, it could not matter less if all the theological tomes in the world and the theologians along with them were burned in one merry bonfire. Rather the collaboration is necessary for the theologian more fully to possess his own theology, to understand it better and make it more pressingly relevant to modern man.

That note brings us to the last point of our considerations: theology after the Council should have one of the characteristics of the Council, namely, a pastoral concern. And here we will be discussing the relevance of theology to the university at long last.

Pastoral concern as related to theology in the context of Catholic higher education must apply to student and faculty alike. What at present might seem to be a pastoral vacuum—a divorce in the Catholic teacher's mind between what he spends his life doing professionally and his gift of faith—can be healed, at least in part, if we help each other return to a vision of the unity of truth. We must share with Origen and Aquinas the realization that when we discover some new truth, rediscover an old truth in a new light, or indeed as teachers present to students an old and even banal truth for the first time, we are dealing with the Primal Truth; we are re-presenting Christ.

This will necessarily call for student and faculty alike to develop a new focus for what we usually call the eyes of faith. We have developed the eyes of faith in terms of the eucharist; we have developed the eyes of faith in terms of seeing Christ in others, particularly in the poor, the disenfranchised, the underprivileged, those forced to live on the periphery of society. Can we not, then, develop the eyes of faith in the area of scholarship, so that we come to see that whenever we lay hold of truth we also lay hold of Christ, and make him in this sense more present in the world? We must develop the tradition of Christian scholarship. But the picture would be incomplete, would it not, if we did not realize that we are dealing with Christ and hence must speak not only of scholarship but also of service? This, too, is to re-present Christ. "I have been among you as one who serves."

A tradition of scholarship and service, then, is necessary if we are effectively to re-present Christ even in our own academic communities. Indeed, some of our present problems can be traced to the fact that in our historic past as educators we have not fully preserved this dual tradition. Is God dead? Or is it only that so many of his followers are, who have supported God with insupportable reasons and, while claiming to believe in a God of Love, have failed to love? Is Christianity dying, or is it that so many of the Christian Churches are dying—dying of entropy, perhaps, a running down of vital energies, because they have trivialized the Good News of the Gospel? The

Churches have often buried the talent in a napkin while they labored
to protect purely institutional interests. The question that many seem
to be asking today is this: are the Churches temples of the living
God wherein he may be found, or are they the empty tombs from
which he has long fled? Are Catholic colleges open to the charge
that they frequently expose the student to Christianity without
Christ—an ironical reversal of the stance of the Christian atheists
who affirm a Christ without Christianity?

I would not want to make my own the warrant for this last question, but I would like to quote from the April 16, 1966, issue of *Ave
Maria*. It contains a letter from a Notre Dame graduate to Father
Hesburgh. We all recognize the wise provision of canon law that no
one can be tried for heresy when the evidence against him is based on
the notes of his student. We also realize that students are not in every
case the best critics of their education. We can go further and agree
with René Descartes that one's dissatisfaction with his education is
indeed a sign that one has been rather well educated. Despite all these
reservations, we cannot afford to ignore the remarks of Mr. Ralph
Martin, Jr., to the president of Notre Dame:

> . . . I graduated magna cum laude, winner of the Dockweiler Award
> in Philosophy, and went to Princeton to study philosophy on a Wood-
> row Wilson. . . .
>
> The first thing that must be mentioned about my experience at
> Notre Dame is that as I was exposed to the best that Notre Dame had
> to offer a student in the College of Arts and Letters, I grew farther
> and farther away from Christianity; it ceased having a practical in-
> fluence in my life. I grew in intellectual ability and in creativity—ex-
> posed to the best professors, the Committee on Academic Progress,
> writing for the *Scholastic* and for the *Juggler*. . . .
>
> These are the small number of Notre Dame faculty who make a
> serious try at relating their academic discipline to Christianity. They
> cannot and do not transmit the Gospel message as it must be pre-
> sented; they cannot and do not confront their students with Jesus
> Christ in the way in which they must if those students are to accept
> or reject Him. . . .
>
> Many of the national fellowship winners in the classes of '64 and '65
> —I know almost every one personally—*are not practicing Catholics*.
> In the course of four years at Notre Dame my own Catholicism dis-
> solved. . . . In my own opinion many of the best students that Notre
> Dames "produces" are no longer Catholics by the time they gradu-
> ate. . . .
>
> Not even a very strong school of theology would change the situa-
> tion very much. The effect on the students, I suspect, would be much

the same as the effect on the deeply Christian teachers—ambiguous and often misleading. For there's a big difference between thinking about Christianity and doing it; and students need to be shown how to do it, asked to do it. They need to be initiated into the Christian life, into a Christian community where the life is being lived in a serious and appropriate liturgy, in a common life of obedience and faith to God's Word openly discussed and acted on, in an apostolic community which is forming men into apostles and saints.

If you would entertain a personal remark, I would like to say this: I am myself a refugee from the academic life. I have taught at three Catholic universities in the United States. And I have known too many students who have been faced with the same problem and have come to the same conclusion as did Ralph Martin to make me feel his letter is entirely chimerical in its description of a pastoral vacuum on the college campus.

Filling that vacuum, I would think, represents the ultimate relevance of theology to the university: helping the people in the university, teachers as well as taught, to recover the vision that focuses the spectrum of truths into one Truth who is a Person. For the Catholic college or university is not only a community of scholars, although it must be that, unmistakably; it is also the Church in miniature, as it were, the community in which the Spirit dwells— that Spirit who is the source and fountain of creative love.

*Communication is the process of creating participation,
of making common what had been isolated and singular;
and part of the miracle it achieves is that,
in being communicated, the conveyance of meaning
gives body and definiteness to the experience
of the one who utters as well as to that of those who listen.*

JOHN DEWEY

BROTHER C. R. WILSON, F.S.C.

2 The Psychology of Communication to a University Mind

Introduction

If one human being wants to communicate with another or with a group, he must have some real understanding of the other person or the group, and he must further communicate this understanding to the other. The understanding ideally should exist at two levels: an objective one, where the competence of the other is recognized and communicated, and a subjective one, where what is communicated carries a note of appreciation or personal approval of the other. These elements must be present prior to any real communication between people, and we will try to examine them along with other constituents of the communication process itself. To ignore these elements would be to destroy the fundaments of interpersonalism.

First let me say that I write as a psychologist and not as a theologian. As I understand my topic, it is to discuss the communication process that takes place between the teacher of sacred doctrine and his students at the college level or higher. As here defined, then, the "university mind" is not the Catholic intellectual or the professional scholar but the student. Also, it is specifically the communication of sacred doctrine that is in question; and the nature of the material to be communicated likewise affects the communication process. Thus, while I do not pretend to be a theologian, yet of necessity I find myself involved with material that is essentially theological. If I venture opinions that have theological implications, it will only be because I am following psychological lines of inquiry to what I think are their natural conclusions. It will be for the teacher to judge the theological aspects. I propose only to present the problems, as I see

them, which accompany the task of trying to teach sacred doctrine
to young people in college.

Communication from the Viewpoint of the Student

It will be helpful to view this communication process from within
the student's internal frame of reference. As he sits in class, he has
two main things to contend with in his efforts to receive the communication: the teacher, who is the sender, and the material to be
communicated, which is the message. His attitudes toward both
teacher and material will have a great deal to do with the message
which he actually receives. Teachers have all at times felt the anguish
of being misquoted, and yet, most times perhaps, the student really
does not feel he is misquoting. The message he received was not the
one that was sent.

In attempting an analysis of these two factors, namely, the teacher
and the material to be communicated, I arrived at the following
scheme of things which I would like first to outline and then to develop.

First, with regard to the teacher, there are two ways in which each
student more or less consciously views him: professionally and personally. By professionally, I mean from the viewpoint that the teacher
of sacred doctrine is a theologian. In other words, he is categorized.
This is not the teacher as this particular theologian with a particular
training and background which would distinguish him from other
theologians. Rather the student consciously or subconsciously refers
all of the general characteristics to the teacher of theology, who
therefore seems like all other theologians in the student's eyes.

Second, there is the teacher as "this theologian," and here is where
his individuality both as a theologian and as a person will play a role
in the readiness with which the student listens to his message. Here is
where the individual's competence as a theologian and his own unique
ways of relating to other people will make themselves felt.

So then, in examining the teacher of sacred doctrine, we will look
at what his profession means to the student, and two elements, very
much related, will emerge as central: authority and freedom.

With regard to the material, the actual content of what is being
taught, there are three major prerequisites to credibility for the modern mind, and these will be examined in turn. The tendency for modern man, including the Catholic college student, is to reject whatever

is not relevant (and this means experiential in some way), relative, and natural.

At first sight, this tendency might seem to present tremendous obstacles to the teaching of theology, but I think that upon closer examination these demands will be seen to represent progress toward a deeper understanding of whatever is true, including theological truths. Where problems are more likely to arise, however, is in the student's lack of understanding of what these requirements for knowledge really mean. They have been gleaned in an atmosphere largely conditioned by the philosophies of existentialism and personalism, by the methods of logical positivism and phenomenology, and by the findings of modern psychology; but all too frequently the deeper meanings of these requirements for knowledge are not really understood by the student. He has only a superficial knowledge of their origins obtained from popularizations and secondary sources, and even these he has hand-picked, frequently choosing only what he likes.

At any rate, we will want to look at these requirements of the material to be communicated—that it be experiential, relative, and natural—along with the professional and personal factors relating to how the instructor is received by the student as a teacher of sacred doctrine.

The Teacher as a Professional Theologian

Let me say again that what we wish to analyze here is the impersonal professional, the teacher as "theologian." As "theologian," he is, in the eyes of the student, an authority. He is an expert on what the Church teaches, and this is more of a liability than an asset. It is not the instructor's personal competence as a theologian that is recognized here; it is rather his role as a spokesman for the Church, a representative of official teaching. The problem this ushers in, of course, is that of authority, and it becomes terribly complicated since it is many-faceted. However, I should like to abstract from extreme individual problems which arise because of the personal background of the student—for example, unresolved problems of parental authority—and look to the more general problem of the Church as a dogmatic authority. There is also the problem of personal background; each one of us has some feelings of hostility or at least opposition to the kind of authority to which we were first subjected by our parents, when

we were told, "Do not do that or you will be punished" and "Do this and you are a good child."

One very prominent theory of communication, formulated by Dr. Milton Rokeach and put forth in his book entitled *The Open and Closed Mind*,[1] is based on the way in which the source of information is viewed as an authority. Rokeach, following Erich Fromm, holds that one drawing from a source of information may view it as a source of truth or well-being for himself, and that this is authority in the benign sense. Such authority seeks to lessen the psychological distance between itself and those who draw from it. It is exemplified in the relationship that exists between the good teacher and his student: the teacher knows something of which the student is ignorant, and after communication has taken place, the shared knowledge has lessened the psychological distance between them.

There is another kind of relationship, however, which seeks to do just the opposite—to increase the psychological distance between the one who exercises so-called authority and the person over whom he has such power. This is exemplified in the relationship which exists between a master and his slave, where interactions between the two are designed to reinforce the slave's state of subservience to the master. Here the threat of punishment, and not the perception of self-improvement, coerces the inferior to conform.

According to Rokeach's theory, each of us has come emotionally to view authority as more or less punishing and more or less demanding of conformity. This is owing to the very early learning of patterns of behavior directed toward parents and other early authority figures. The more one is inclined to view authority as rewarding and punishing and therefore demanding compliance, the more dogmatic he is in his thinking, according to Dr. Rokeach. Such a person's beliefs are largely unreasoned and are maintained through fear. The less a person views authority as punishing and the more he sees authority as serving or contributing to his well-being, the more open, or less dogmatic, he is in his thinking.

Apart from the individual who reflects a severe degree of dogmatic thinking and who admittedly has his problems because of the predispositions of his own perceptual system, we are all more or less dogmatic in this emotional sense of the word as used by Rokeach. The result is that if an authority presents itself as punishing and as de-

[1] Milton Rokeach, *The Open and Closed Mind*, New York, Basic Books, 1960, Chap. 1.

manding compliance, then even the average well-adjusted person will rebel in some way against that authority. It is even healthy to do so. Of course, we can see the problems immediately: because of human abuses or at least human failures, much unhealthy dogmatism has been exercised in the Church by some churchmen.

The cause has largely been the emergence in past centuries of a cultic view of the priesthood, which led clergy and especially bishops to withdraw into their ivory towers, fancying themselves professional administrators of the sacraments and keepers of the collective conscience of the mystical body. It is not surprising that the faithful came to regard them as the powerful controlling body within the Church and therefore as a coercive force. The relationship of clergy to people was further complicated by the fact that the bishop considered the priest himself to occupy a subservient position: the relationship between the priest and his bishop was specified by obedience and dependence. As a result, an authoritarian power structure developed within the Church whereby pronouncements came from the top down. Though the priest was considered the lowest element in that power structure, he was nonetheless part of the ruling body, and was thus looked upon by the laity as a constrictive and coercive force.

What has all this to do with theology and theologians? Actually, a great deal. Theology, after all, is bound up with the so-called official teaching of the Church in the eyes of the layman, and theologians are the voices which preach the "party line." The point I am trying to make is simply that the power structure within the ministerial priesthood has evoked many rebellious feelings from the laity, and these are frequently displaced onto theology viewed as Church teaching. Some might argue that the college student is more knowledgeable; but we cannot forget that his emotional background with reference to the Church is much the same as that of his parents, with the one notable exception that given continued social and religious growth within the culture, he is less afraid to question, to reject, and even to rebel against what he sees as Church authoritarianism.

Gregory Baum has pointed out that Vatican II has laid the foundation for an understanding of the ministerial priesthood which will allow for shared responsibility and a participation on the part of priests in the determination of policy. He says:

> The new understanding of the ministerial priesthood offers a doctrinal foundation for a kind of collegiality between the bishop and his

priests. Collegiality in its proper sense between pope and bishops has its foundation in the unity of the episcopal college; collegiality in a wider sense between the bishop and his priests has its doctrinal basis in the common participation in the ministerial priesthood, the bishop fully, and the priests in a limited and dependent manner.[2]

But until the ecclesiastical image changes radically in the eyes of the world, this tension will continue to exist, and of necessity the opposition to authoritarianism will generalize to theology. It seems clear that the power structure within the Church must change if the rift between Catholicism and the secular world is not to end in total alienation.

It is unfortunately true that Western culture tends to equate authority with authoritarianism, and consequently authority is seen as a detriment to personal freedom. It will only be through a proper use of authority within the Church that the basic conditions for the communication of God's revelation of Himself will be established. Father Congar maintains that we are moving toward a proper understanding of authority when we see it in relation to two fundamental religious realities:

> They are the living God acting among us through his grace, and the holy community and brotherhood of the faithful. It is by setting authority in an authentic relationship with these two Christian realities that we shall be able to go beyond legalism which consists in seeing the formal validity of phenomena without penetrating to their meaning.[3]

Of course, it takes but a few members of the hierarchy to demonstrate amply that this rigid power structure still can operate in such a way as to make authority in the Church domination rather than service and charity. The problem is further complicated by the fact that the process of secularization, of which Harvey Cox speaks, is advancing at breakneck speed, and if immediate measures are not taken to facilitate genuine communication between hierarchy and priests and between priests and people, dire consequences will result. We cannot expect the modern mind to accept hierarchical pronouncements or directives that seem to flow from senility or prejudice or emotional imbalance. Bishops can no longer expect unthinking compliance from their priests, any more than priests

[2] Gregory Baum, "The Ministerial Priesthood," *The Ecumenist*, November-December, 1965, p. 7.

[3] Yves Congar, O.P., *Power and Poverty in the Church*, Baltimore, Helicon Press, 1964, p. 78.

can demand it from their parishioners. If the power structure does not adapt itself, the Church risks fading into insignificance as a positive force for molding society, at least in our time.

I do not think that this point concerning authoritarianism can be overstressed; it is one of the major obstacles to communicating theology to the student. It is important also to realize that practically all of us were trained under an authoritarian system. Priests are not alone in manifesting a "clerical mentality"; brothers and sisters, too, are likely to fall victim to its stifling force within their respective societies, as well as to the fallacy that the secular world ought to accord us special favors by reason of the respect we deserve as religious. I am told that since the number of Irish policemen is dropping, more and more priests and brothers (I do not know about sisters) are getting speeding tickets. Well, I honestly think that we deserve the ordinary respect and consideration from the police that any good citizen deserves, and no more. We should not expect the garb to immunize us from ordinary sanctions.

I consider Harvey Cox's description of the process of secularization to be an accurate sociological account of what is taking place. If we are to participate in building the secular city, we must accept its basic tenets. We cannot afford to separate ourselves from the world which is present to us if we wish to be a positive force in its creation. Religious orders, in particular those of women, will have to adapt radically, especially in their power structures, if they are to be maintained at all. The psychologically healthy young man or woman who is the product of the secular city will not accept medieval practices on the basis that they are according to God's will. All these elements contribute to the image of obsolescence that is coming more and more to be associated with the Church.

The Teacher as an Individual

Turning now to the teacher as an individual, I should like to pass over the matter of professional competency. It is a very important one, but I think it suffices here to assume that a professional teacher realizes his training is a lifelong process. In other words, he is not only well trained in theology but keeps up with his field.

When it comes to the teacher as a person who has his own peculiar ways of relating to people, this is another matter. If he has imbibed enough authoritarianism from his early training in religion and has not since had enough normal life experience to bounce back from the trauma, then he may present himself as a very authoritarian and rigid person to the students. In this case, no matter how good a theologian he may be, his communication with them will be at best garbled. Unless he can listen to them, understand their difficulties, and show that he understands them, he will never communicate accurately what he wants to say to them. Probably also, since he will not be inclined to discuss issues with them, even though he and they may talk to each other in what superficially appears to be dialogue, he will not really reach them.

The modern college or university student is not ready to accept authoritative teaching in the area of religion. Most of them are vitally interested in anything which bears on their personal lives and very uninterested in what they view as outmoded concepts which nobody believes anyway. If they see a teacher as behind the times or out of touch, they will copy his notes to get the credit and nothing more.

Actually, the better the theologian is able to relate to students individually and to see his classes not as mere instruction periods but as communal life experiences, the greater will be the influence of the theological insights he shares with them. If he becomes for them a sacrament of encounter with Christ, Who in turn is the sacrament of encounter with the Father, then he will be bringing God to the secular city. But a good deal of the mystery lies in the fact that he effectively does this only insofar as he is genuinely human, genuinely personal—in a word, truly himself.

Requirements for Credibility

Finally, let us consider the requirements for credibility which I mentioned earlier: relevance, relativity, and naturalness.

As I said earlier, the college student discounts information which he does not see as relevant, that is, as bearing on his life. A television commercial for Dial soap that offers "round-the-clock protection" may well be more relevant to the life of a given student than the particular religious truth he happens to be learning; and if this is the way he sees it, the commercial will have a positive influence but the teacher's message will not. I do not think an instructor should try to force theological concepts into unlikely practical molds, but as a professional theologian he can, I should imagine, refer molecular truths back to more global ones which do positively bear on the lives of the students. Where he cannot present the material as relevant, he will of necessity fail.

Moreover, for the material to be relevant, students must be able to refer it to their own experience. A teacher might say, "Well, that's too bad. They just have to learn that the intellectual content of theology often doesn't have any experiential point of contact." If this is the case, then as a psychologist I must honestly tell you that such content will not be learned by the student. Whether or not things should be this way is beside the point; the fact is that they are.

The view of God as immanent rather than as a being-out-there appeals to the modern mind. In fact, talk enough about the transcendent God, the prime mover, and so forth, and you feed into the other popular belief of the student—that this God, at least, is dead.

I am not qualified to judge how good Karl Barth is as a theologian, but I have been very impressed by the way he uses the material of theology in appealing to the modern mentality. He proceeds phenomenologically, after positing the need for revelation if we are to know anything about God at all. From the outset, he takes only the data of revelation, and refuses to fall back upon concepts that spring from so-called natural theology. While he speaks of God always in interpersonal terms, seeing Him as the *I* Who reveals Himself to man and Who is therefore intramundane, he insists that Saint Thomas is correct in seeing God as a *principium extrinsecum* if He is to be recognizable from the world He created. But Barth also insists that this supramundane God can be known by man only to the degree that He reveals Himself as World-ruler, as indeed He does in and through Christ in the New Testament. In this approach Barth sees no need for a second postulate, namely, whether or not this extramundane God and World-ruler exists. He says:

> The basis is the intramundane self-demonstration of the extramundane God and World-ruler. And dogmatics has to take over this naivety and strength in its own thinking and utterance. There is no alternative if it is to be Christian thinking and utterance. If we are really to have a World-ruler, one who is capable of world dominion as *principium extrinsecum*, we have to relate the matter to the King of Israel.[4]

I am not trying to theologize; I use this only as an example of what appears to me to be a valid approach. It is noteworthy that Barth insists on the existence of a transcendent God while at the same time acknowledging that we can know God experientially only in terms of His immanence, of His self-revelation.

To move on to the second condition of credibility—that state-

[4] Karl Barth, *Church Dogmatics,* New York, Harper & Brothers, 1961, p. 35.

ments of truth are relative—it might be well to start by recognizing
the basic validity of this thesis. Even *de fide* pronouncements of the
Church are expressed in all too contingent words. As human beings
we search after absolutes, but any knowledge we arrive at will always be clothed in language, and the meanings will therefore be
limited and changeable. We do not know absolutes, although we
may know about them. So the teacher in any field, and especially in
theology, who speaks in terms of "the last word" on the subject immediately sets up obstacles to the credibility of his message.

The student may not be able to say why such statements are unac-
ceptable, but he has been reared in an atmosphere of logical positivism and phenomenology, and somehow instinctively he rebels against
such absolute certitude. Once again, this is the way things are, and if
a teacher wants really to communicate with the modern youngster,
he must begin by accepting him just as he is. Moreover, I think the
student is right, and that theology itself has much to gain from realizing the full implications of the relativity of language.

Of course, this is nothing new to the field of sacred doctrine; I
realize that leading Catholic theologians are speaking of demythologizing religious beliefs and of the need for a transcendental anthropology in order to understand man in his relationship with God. All
of this is good from the viewpoint of making theology meaningful
to the modern college or university student. It is equally essential
for the teacher of sacred doctrine to realize that man's understanding
of truth, even theological truth, is in a constant process of evolution
and refinement. Even the Church herself is in evolution. Theologians
like Johann B. Metz see the importance of a futuristic orientation to
God and His truth. It seems that we are being told from all sides that
we must embrace the fullness of truth which we now possess without falling into the error of thinking that what we have has exhausted the possibilities of God's revelation to us.

And finally, we come to the third requirement for credibility—
naturalness. The modern mind refuses to accept theoretical dichotomies which cannot be demonstrated. A supernatural reality that
exists outside of man's experience has no essential meaning for
modern man since he has come to know so much about nature and
to place such confidence in its marvels.

Dichotomies like the severance of body from soul make no sense
to him either, and such concepts as intellect and will are frequently
seen as outmoded theoretical constructs. Yet I do not believe that

modern man has lost either his sense of mystery or his capacity to revere what he does see as true. Harvey Cox maintains that with the rise of a pluralistic society, we must educate our young people to uncertainty:

> If change and ceaseless readjustment will be needed in the world of tomorrow, and if the Church is called to contribute to the health of the world, Christians must be free from depending on fixed props and standard scenery. The pilgrim character of the Church must apply not only to places, but to thought forms. We must be mentally mobile enough to move on to the next spot without weeping to return to emotional Egypts.[5]

The three requirements for credibility are interrelated, of course. For example, what is accepted as natural today will not be a hundred years from now, because there is a relativity of knowledge and we shall know much more about nature a century hence. It follows also that what man considers relevant at the mid-twenty-first century will therefore be quite different from what we see as relevant to our era.

One thing seems certain: the modern demands are such that theology will have to be creative or it will not survive as a field of knowledge. It is encouraging that our leading theologians are meeting the challenge, and they never cease to amaze laymen like myself with their fresh approaches. But the changes are confusing, and here the teacher of theology must come to our aid. He must show his students the way to live in Christ in the secular city, and in effect bring that city to Christ. We can no longer say with Augustine that ". . . two cities have been built by two loves: the earthly by the love of self, even to the contempt of God; the heavenly by the love of God, even to the contempt of self." [6] We must rather say of the secular city that one city is being built by one love—God's love for us. By our response of faith to that love will the inhabitants of the secular city attain to the maturity of love for one another which characterizes the mystical body in all ages. For this, we must accept the secular city, grow with it, and consecrate it through the sacramentality of our own love for others.

[5] Harvey Cox, "Secularization and the Secular Mentality: A New Challenge to Christian Education," *Religious Educator*, March-April, 1966, p. 87.
[6] Saint Augustine, *The City of God*, tr. Marcus Dods, New York, Modern Library, 1950, p. 477, Bk. XIV, Chap. 28.

In a period of turbulence, both in individual lives
and in the life of history, the church points to its symbols
which show that despite restlessness and chaos
there is an ultimate rest. . . . Today when I think
of the generation in colleges and universities,
this seems to be the most important message
we can give them. In a disintegrating society, in the loss
of symbols, in cynicism and the terrible feeling of emptiness,
the church should show that there is another dimension to
existence, there is still a source of fullness and meaning and
of truth.

PAUL TILLICH

BROTHER C. STEPHEN SULLIVAN, F.S.C.

3   The Dimensions of Theology in
a Catholic College in the Light of Vatican II

Although it would be much more prudent for me to write as a teacher of theology, I am rash enough to be wearing the administrator's hat as I reflect on the dimensions of theology in the Catholic college in the light of Vatican II. I hope you will be patient with me as I return to a method of my teaching days—and somewhat of my theologian days—while I consider the subject at hand according to four rather obvious divisions: dimensions, theology, the Catholic college, and the Second Vatican Ecumenical Council.

The fourfold dimensions of length, width, depth, and—to borrow from science fiction—time suggest four specific questions: What is the scope of the theology curriculum which should be offered? What limitations should be placed on the areas selected for study? How profound should the study be? And what constant changes must be envisioned in structuring a theology program?

Today our colleges in general insist that we are engaged in a theological endeavor. Serious and very commendable efforts are being made by the Commission on Religion in Higher Education of the Association of American Colleges to foster the study of religion in higher education, an aim shared by the Danforth Foundation, the Society for Religion in Higher Education, and the Religious Education Association. But more deeply and specifically, we are concerned with the study of *theology* in higher education, a term quite different from *religion* because it includes a confessional commitment. Moreover, this difference plays a major role in the identity crisis, a problem which is believed to be looming large in many Catholic colleges. In great measure the problem arises because these schools are growing alongside the great secular learning centers of the country.

It seems axiomatic to say that the Catholic college in the United States today is facing many difficulties—including extinction. In fact, a recent edition of *Look* magazine carried an article which suggested that the end of Catholic education's reason for existence in this country is in sight. The author says that the converging movements of ecumenism, the Catholic's attitude toward the environment in which he lives, and the increasing expressions of freedom and pluralism in Catholic education are effecting such changes that soon there will be no need for the separate Catholic college. The same article states:

> The final paradox of this situation is that in the judgment of Catholic educators who have moved farthest in response to it, the real crisis for Catholic education lies far beyond clericalism, lay control, freedom or even academic excellence. What haunts them [Catholic educators] is the thought that even if Catholic schools are able to solve their problems in these areas, they will only have brought themselves face to face with another and even more serious question, which is: Why should Catholic colleges exist at all? [1]

The crisis of identity for the Catholic college is very real; it is apparent when attempts are made to distinguish the developed modern Catholic university and college from the secular institutions. Indeed, some of the actions and statements of certain Catholic educators seem to suggest that they seriously question the need for a Catholic college.

The dilemma found in the identity crisis is partially at the root of the question being raised about the role of clergy and religious in conducting Catholic colleges. Actually, to some it may appear that there is a kind of power struggle going on between the lay faculty and the clerical and/or religious faculty. I do not believe this is the case. The question we are facing is, who is best equipped to do the job. It is not a matter of emerging laymen versus submerging clergy, but who can best preserve the ideals of significant intellectual inquiry in the Catholic college.

The identity crisis is also complicated by the opinions and attitudes of students, faculty, alumni, the professional staff in areas such as development, and "the administration." (This term usually has the

---

[1] Richard Horchler, "The Time Bomb in Catholic Education," *Look*, April 5, 1966, p. 25.

definite article and is almost always used by campus groups in the third person. As an administrator, I often feel like a member of the caste system—in fact, an untouchable.)

There seem to be as many ideas of what a college should be as there are students. Faculties vary according to their disciplines; their approach to the concept of what the college is or should be is largely dictated by the type of thinking which characterizes their own specialty. Even the departmental structure of American higher education has raised barriers between the various segments of a faculty, and has made it more difficult for a faculty to agree on what a Catholic college ought to be. Alumni sometimes seem to be regarded as romantic, sentimental groups who can be tolerated but who are not to be taken too seriously in academic affairs. They must be satisfied or deceived into thinking that the college today is worthy of support. On the other hand, alumni do represent traditional thinking in an institution, and this can be ignored only at the price of daring to ignore history. Development people are asked to do a specialized kind of marketing job and to help create and project our "images." They find it difficult to understand why the wheels of an academic institution grind so slowly.

In all these areas, the Catholic college must contend with a great variety of factors. In this they share the same problems which all institutions of higher learning must face, but the situation is further complicated because each of these groups conceives of the institution in a different way; their myriad views of the nature of a Catholic college compound the confusion. Yet, underlying all these complications is the identity crisis—the problem of what a Catholic college is, what distinguishes it, and why it is needed.

The Vatican Council has given us some illuminating answers to these questions. With regard to the teaching of theology in the Catholic college, the synod has highlighted the areas which are most significant for the curriculum, and it has created a milieu which should permeate the approach of teacher and student. It is now almost trite to say that college theology should be biblical, liturgical, and ecumenical. After the Council, college theology must include a study of the Church, revelation, personal freedom, and the social questions facing the world today.

However, this does not mean a complete revamping of what we have been doing. There can be no understanding of any of these areas unless the doctrine of the Incarnation remains as the focal point of our investigations: from the Incarnation flow the Church, the liturgy, the sacraments, the presence of Christ in today's world. In fact, there is a danger that such topics will be treated as separate entities, without reference to the Incarnation. This prospect is frightening because it threatens to generate a pseudo-Christian sociology or, even worse, a compromise with the reality of Jesus Christ, the Word Incarnate. A failure to show how the work of the Council is rooted in the Incarnation can lead students to embrace Appalachia projects or join the civil rights struggle on a purely secular basis; it tends to create the mentality which uproots the dignity of man from the essential concept of God's presence in this world. The Council's statements give us directions for emphasis, but they do not change completely the fundamental commitments we must examine in our theology courses.

What is the milieu created by the council which we should seek to communicate to our students? It is a fearless openmindedness. Throughout the Council there was manifested a humble confidence which grew out of the commitment of faith; with this confidence grew a fearlessness on the part of the Council Fathers to face even the most difficult problems, a wonderful tolerance of the limitations of the creature's ability to resolve all questions, and a glorious flexibility which enabled the Fathers to develop their utterances so as to embrace the truth wherever it was to be found. The Council's actions should serve as a model for all Catholic colleges and universities to emulate.

However, all is not serene. John O'Connor, director of the Catholic Press Association, has pointed out:

> The raging controversies that mark the Church's landscape are not our private squabble: rather, our agony of ferment and reform and renewal belongs to the world. It became the world's when Pope John threw open the windows and invited observers in; it became the world's when he asked that journalists spread the news of the Council; it became the world's with Paul's pilgrimages of involvement to the long-alienated East, to the poor of India and to the world powers at the United Nations. You cannot contain a revolution that is moved by an idea. And the idea that has caught fire among many Catholics— Council Fathers, "new breed" priests, wave after wave of seminarians and newly awakened laymen—is the idea that the Church is a people on the move, and that Christ is going to get a hearing in the modern world *only* if we who are baptized listen to the Holy Spirit speaking through the Council, and act.
> The Four Horsemen of the Resistance ride the hill country of the

Catholic backwoods: provincialism, Jansenism, authoritarianism, and clericalism. Against these an emerging generation makes war.[2]

Father Pedro Arrupe, newly elected Superior General of the Society of Jesus, also gave testimony to the upheaval effected by the Council in his sermon on Palm Sunday, 1966, in the Church of St. Ignatius in New York. Father Arrupe said:

> Many Catholics are afraid of this new world that seems to have descended upon us so suddenly, so violently. For, as they see it, it is a world where the machine has replaced man, liberty has supplanted law, doubt has driven out certainty; where the Church herself seems in such constant ferment and inner torment that the simple Catholic is confused and the sophisticated Catholic is highly critical; when all the things we took for granted, that made human living so serene, have been questioned, turned inside out, subjected to radical revision; where 2,500 bishops gathered in council have given Catholics not the answers they were hoping for, but fresh problems.
>
> At the risk of startling you, let me tell you quite honestly, it is not this new world that I fear. . . . I am rather afraid that we Jesuits may have little or nothing to offer this world, little or nothing to say or do that would justify our existence as Jesuits.
>
> I am afraid that we may repeat yesterday's answers to tomorrow's problems, talk in a way men no longer understand, speak a language that does not speak to the heart of living man. If we do this, we shall more and more be talking to ourselves; no one will listen, because no one understands what we are trying to say.

I believe the message is clear. Vatican II has been a magnificent experience, a thrilling spectacle—but it has violently changed our way of life and thinking. In fact, we have not yet seen the total implications of the Council, because we are still too close to it. The next phase of the Council's accomplishments is beginning—and I believe it will be an arduous period of uncertainty and confusion.

Now that we have considered the terms used in the title of this paper (amounting to a kind of *status quaestionis*), I would like to formulate a question and suggest some answers. My question is: How extensive, how broad, and how deep should theological instruction be to insure that it is a principal distinguishing note of a Catholic college in the confused postconciliar period? The question is complicated because of the specifications I have made in my comments

[2] John O'Connor, "Controversy Within the Church," *America*, April 9, 1966, p. 483.

on its various parts. I state apologetically that my answer will be oversimplified.

I will broach my answer by saying that the Catholic college should deliberately teach *theology*, by which I understand an academic discipline which begins with our confessional commitment and in which our human mind explores the total implications of this confessional stance. What should the dimensions of this study be? Rather than try to answer in terms of a specific curriculum, may I suggest that the study extend to an intellectual journey which is characterized by the openmindedness manifested in Vatican II. Our theological investigation will be complete only after we have conveyed to our students an appreciation of the value of exploring the Christian faith (as it is proposed by the Catholic Church) with a sense of commitment, a spirit of tolerance, and a flexible modality. Our task is to transmit truth as we see it and in a manner consonant with the times in which we live.

I believe that such a theological study should be the distinguishing characteristic of a Catholic college. In it I include not only the course offerings of a theology department but also the contributions made by other departments which show the relations between other disciplines and the Christian commitment. To my mind, Catholic colleges exist in order to examine a definite commitment. I maintain that we will continue to flounder in the identity crisis until we proclaim to all our publics that this is our reason for existence. Moreover, public proclamation is not enough. We must make specific efforts to educate our various constituencies (faculty, students, administrators, alumni) to understand that the way we fulfill this mission will always be subject to change and development. Our only constant characteristic should be that we will freely seek to attain greater knowledge in all areas, and that this knowledge will always be examined and criticized in relation to the Christian commitment.

How must this theological endeavor be conducted in the light of Vatican II? My answers, once again, are simple. Multiple efforts must be made to analyze the conciliar documents and to incorporate them into ongoing curricula. Special workshops, forums, and other types of discussion groups should be held to deepen understanding of the documents. Most important of all, the Council's great openmindedness should mold theology teaching in the Catholic college. Let us avoid labels like *liberal* and *conservative*. Let us avoid the irresponsible approaches of the sophisticated critic who becomes a kind of intellectual mad bomber. Let us make dedicated and conscious efforts to manifest commitment, tolerance, and flexibility.

In 1965 Manning Pattillo and Donald MacKenzie, Associate Directors of the Danforth Foundation, published their *Preliminary Report of the Danforth Commission on Church Colleges and Universities*. The concluding chapter states that Church-related colleges in this country tend to fall into three classes or models: "defenders of the faith colleges," "non-affirming colleges," and "free Christian colleges." The first type is "usually controlled by single denominations but sometimes by evangelical or fundamentalist groups that cut across denominational lines. Their constituents usually contribute financial support which is large in relation to their number and means. In return they expect that the institutions will safeguard the faith and even the social practices of the community." [3] The non-affirming college, though Church-related, is an institution which gives relatively little formal attention to religion. "Neither students nor faculty are attracted to the college because of its church connection. Students are admitted and faculty appointed without regard to religious interest or belief. The catalogue and other publications make brief mention of the church affiliation, but the statement of educational purposes is likely to omit any reference to religion or to speak in more general terms of moral and spiritual values." [4]

The third model, the free Christian college,

. . . is free because it does not control thought, Christian because it has a definite commitment. Most of its faculty share its religious purposes and consider them to be important in the life of the college. Students are attracted by the dual emphasis on academic excellence and religious vitality. The college surrounds its students with opportunities for full development—intellectual, religious, moral, artistic, social.

While Chapel attendance may not be required, the Chapel is a focal point of student and faculty interest. Worship is viewed as important. The department of religion is composed of well-trained teachers who play an active role in faculty affairs. The courses in religion are rigorous and stimulating and are an integral part of the academic program. The college does not tell its students what they should believe, but it does expect them to grapple with basic religious and philosoph-

[3] Manning M. Pattillo, Jr., and Donald M. MacKenzie, *Eight Hundred Colleges Face the Future: A Preliminary Report of the Danforth Commission on Church Colleges and Universities*, St. Louis, Danforth Foundation, 1965, pp. 68-69.
[4] *Ibid.*, p. 69.

ical questions and try to arrive at a position of their own. Much attention is given to the relationship between religion and intellectual problems of our day. Religion and liberal learning are regarded as mutually supportive.

The Danforth report recommends that this third model be widely adopted. It "combines the assets of the other models while it tries to avoid their liabilities. It stands unapologetically for religion and liberal education, but it relies on example, persuasive presentation of ideas, and a climate of conviction rather than on conformity to accomplish its ends." [5]

I believe that this model is most in keeping with the spirit of Vatican II. I endorse it and recommend it to your thinking as an ideal situation in which the theological endeavor can flourish in our age.

[5] *Ibid.*, p. 69.

*Lord Acton, the English historian, has said that the
concept of freedom, as we know it in our civilization,
rests upon the Hebrew-Christian conviction of an area of
inviolate freedom at the heart of every person. . . .
The same must be said of every primary group
which nurtures the person. Its health depends upon
its capacity to sustain creative criticism and prophetic
judgment within its own ranks.*

CHARLES R. STINNETTE, JR.

REVEREND JOSEPH A. TRAVERS, O.S.F.S.

4   The Limits of Student Protests for Peace, and Freedom for Clergy and Religious

One of the thorniest problems confronting the college administrator, professor, and student today is that of student protests: groups organized to protest certain real or seeming injustices. We have heard them referred to as "angry young men," "Vietniks," "peaceniks," even semi-politely as "pacifists."

They have been psychoanalyzed, studied by the sociologist, traced to their origins by the historian; and the politician has defended or condemned them according to his needs of the moment. The theologian must also face up to the existence of these groups. He must try to relate them to their ultimate destiny. He will see them primarily as "images of God." He will strive to channel their energies accordingly. It is evident, I believe, that there is no solution applicable to every case. Nevertheless, we should attempt to find some guidelines, not merely to keep "the institution" in smooth operating condition but more to educate the student to the proper notion of freedom and responsibility and to a proper use of these.

Freedom is the most basic of all man's rights. It springs directly from his rationality. Negatively, freedom is held to mean that a man may not be forced to act against his convictions or be restricted in acting according to them. Positively, and more importantly, it means that a man will be given the full opportunity to develop his whole potential.

But any man is more than an individual, an isolated unit. He is a person; he is social. He grasps the interpersonal quality of his rights. He realizes that his own freedom cannot be a human right and inalienable unless it belongs to all members of his species. Once he isolates himself and his rights, he loses his personal quality and destroys his rights. Any man, then, must recognize his dependence by his very nature on other men. The history of man is the story of his struggle to be fully man. To guarantee his basic freedom, he forms a society. The basic society, whether it be a tribe or a complex modern state, can lay claim to a right to existence and authority only on the basis of protecting the rights of the individual. The common good is nothing more than the protection of the rights of the individual. The Fathers of Vatican II have declared: "The common welfare of society consists in the entirety of those conditions of social life under which men enjoy the possibility of achieving their own perfection in a certain fullness of measure and also with some relative ease. Hence, this welfare consists chiefly in the protection of the rights, and in the performance of the duties, of the human person." [1]

And now, let's go back to our meddlesome students. They, too, are persons endowed with all human rights. Like any other segment of humanity, they may form groupings; they may organize for some need that they feel they can fulfill better as a group than as individuals. Perhaps a group of students want physical exercise, and so they form a baseball team. These individual members determine the need. Perhaps they then discover that the college has ample facilities to fulfill their desire; so they disband. No special reason, no team. So, too, some students see the occasion to rectify some injustice. In the first instance, they determine that this is a need, and so they organize. Sometimes the need is only apparent, and so the students have no objective goal. Thus, they should disband, or if necessary be disbanded by the proper authority. Only too often do we find students clamoring for better means of communication with the administration when the available channels approach perfection but have never been tried. Occasionally students raise a storm over some real injustice without realizing that it could be speedily rectified simply by reporting it to the proper authority. They really acquire no right to organize a protest since a prior right exists in the proper authority.

Nevertheless, as long as a need is seen to exist and the contrary is not evident or proven, and a group aspires to fulfill that need,

---

[1] Declaration on Religious Freedom, tr. John Courtney Murray, S.J., in Walter M. Abbott, S.J., ed., *The Documents of Vatican II,* New York, America Press, 1966, pp. 683-684, sec. 6.

such a group, whether athletic, cultural, social, industrial, or any other, has a right to exist and to strive for the fulfillment of this need. The individual can achieve many goals in concert with his fellow men that he cannot achieve alone. Students therefore have the right to organize in groups to rectify an injustice, and they have the right to the means to achieve this goal. In *Pacem in terris* Pope John tells us: "From the fact that human beings are by nature social, there arises the right of assembly and association. They have also the right to give the societies of which they are members the form they consider most suitable for the aim they have in view, and to act within such societies on their own initiative and on their own responsibility in order to achieve their desired objectives." [2] The word *right* indicates that others must respect the freedom of this group to exist and to achieve its goal, and that they may not arbitrarily disallow the group or restrict its means. If there is to be any limitation of this right, it must be judged in relation to the need itself or the means employed by the group.

It goes without saying that the need must be in accord with the ultimate destiny of man. To organize a group for purely immoral purposes, for example, for filthy language, could hardly be termed a need for a creature destined for a life with God.

All human law, whether civil or ecclesiastical, should be in harmony with the final destiny of man. In fact, civil society exists simply to guarantee man the necessary freedom to develop his potential in this life, even though such society may not always realize that the full development of man's potential lies beyond its scope. The state can and must make regulations for the sake of public order, and it may use sanctions to enforce these laws. Now, if the purpose for which a student group is formed is not in conformity with civil law, that purpose is presumed to be immoral. A group organized for gambling purposes in a state where this has been judged illegal cannot acquire rights.

It may happen that a particular statute or its execution can be shown to be unjust. Such a statute then loses its moral force. Many of the civil rights groups are and should be free to exist, even though they contravene certain laws in a given area. In some cases, the law is manifestly unjust; in others, the law itself is just but its execution is

[2] *Pacem in terris*, in *Seven Great Encyclicals*, Glen Rock, N.J., Paulist Press, 1963, pp. 293-294, sec. 23.

unjust in that it is not equally applied to all. It would seem that the various groups protesting foreign policy are not contravening any civil legislation regarding their goal.

The Church, too, has its human laws; and the same principles apply. In a particular instance, it may happen that an ecclesiastical superior may put forth some regulation that is unjust; it cries out for rectification. If we are to believe the daily papers, the teachers and students protesting the situation at Saint John's University may well have been justified. But perhaps the Public Relations Department could use an overhaul.

The case of a silenced or transferred priest or other religious is far more involved. The problem of freedom within the ranks of the Church was not clarified by Vatican II. In wartime, it would be treasonous to protest an officer's demotion or transfer. Some feel that the priest is an officer always leading the Christian soldiery in its struggle. There is no legislation on this point; but with such a reverence for the Reverend, who needs legislation?

The priest or other religious must consider the present attitude of the people. Whether officially or not, he is often taken as spokesman for his Church. Disobedience will sometimes scandalize the "little ones." If, in his conscience, he feels that he is being treated unjustly and recourse to higher authority has no changing effect, even then he would do well not to encourage protests. The brilliance of the great Cardinal Newman was not dimmed because he bowed before questionable authority. Nor was his sanctity.

What about the students who take it upon themselves to protest in favor of such a priest? As in civil law, it must be presumed that the order is just, unless the contrary can be shown. Admittedly, a superior may abuse his authority. But who is to determine this? A bishop may forbid a particular priest to demonstrate because he realizes that this particular individual may do more harm than good. It would be well for all of us and our students to read Chesterton's "The Chief Mourner of Marne." [3] Students should be wary in demonstrating for the freedom of priests and other religious, unless there is evident injustice involved. Nonetheless, in the absence of any clarification of freedom within the Church, I do not think we should

---

[3] In G. K. Chesterton, *Father Brown Omnibus*, New York, Dodd, Mead & Co., 1951, pp. 522-535.

say *a priori* that students or anyone else cannot acquire rights to demonstrate even against ecclesiastical authority.

The means employed by such groups must, like the end or need, be in conformity with divine and human law. Suicide, a direct violation of God's law, cannot be considered a legitimate means of protest. Likewise, acts violating civil law ordinarily would be presumed to be against the common welfare and therefore immoral. Draft card burning, for example, is a violation of civil law. If the protesters believe this is an unjust law, they should try to point out this fact of injustice. In many cases, however, it seems that they admit such a law to be legitimate in itself, but feel that they may flout it because of a greater good. An immoral means is not justified by a good end.

In judging whether or not there is any limitation of either ends or means, it must be kept in mind that the judgment should be made on the substance of the group and not upon some accidental element. A group should not be suppressed because one member is immoral, or even worse a "radical," whatever that is!

According to the foregoing, then, it follows that as long as a group of protesters have a legitimate need and use legitimate means to achieve the fulfillment of that need, the group acquire a right to exist and a right to use such means. No human authority may arbitrarily disallow or restrict the freedom of such organizations, because human society and authority exist precisely to protect and guarantee this basic right of the person, individually and socially.

Not only should such groups not be abolished or unduly limited; they should be properly encouraged. More than ever we require the prophet arousing the conscience of the people. We are not yet a perfect people. The good Pope John tells us, "It is most necessary that a wide variety of societies or intermediate bodies be established, equal to the task of accomplishing what the individual cannot by himself efficiently achieve." He states that "These societies are to be regarded as an indispensable means in safeguarding the dignity and liberty of the human person, without harm to his sense of responsibility." [4]

Now we arrive at the real moral core of the problem: not negative legalistic restriction, but positive, Christlike responsibility. If a meaningful moral evaluation is to be made, it must be made from within

---

[4] *Pacem in terris*, p. 294, sec. 24.

the group itself and by its members. The group should be treated as an association of human persons; they should respond to this freedom as human persons. They acquire their rights as persons. As noble crusaders, they accept the challenge to rectify injustice. They are the true champions of human dignity. God be with them! May he never let them forget their human dignity made to his own image; may he never let them lose sight of their magnificent vision. May they ever keep in the forefront of their minds that the moment they deny or limit freedom to another, they are denying the very basis of that right for themselves. They have the right to express their grievances and hopes; so do others. They have the right to their property, corporate and private; so do others.

As mature college students, we can confidently hope, they will employ that most noble intellectual virtue of prudence in determining their forms of protest, which will almost necessarily infringe upon the rights of others. And even when they may justly have prior rights, this prudence will dictate caution. It is so easy for an association of human persons—the protesters themselves as well as others—to become an inhuman herd. As intellectuals, or at least intelligent beings, they should address themselves to man's intelligence, not to his weakness, prejudices, passions, and fears. Above all, we pray that they not confuse their interpretation of facts with divine inerrancy. It takes a large soul for one to admit that he may have been mistaken. In short, the challenge is a most noble one; the responsibility should not make us give up. "The charity of Christ urges us onward." If we all hold fast to the true charity of Christ, we have no call to fear.

When the Christian teacher has drawn some guidelines in this matter, has he really done enough? The teacher, even the moralist, must help lead souls to their complete fulfillment. The guidelines must be shown as relevant to the development of the person. They must be shown as beacons, not as chains. Freedom must not be depicted as something to be tolerated under certain circumstances, but rather as something absolutely essential to all men. Responsibility must not be taught as the burden of the powerful few; it must be expected of every being worthy of the title *person*. Our duty as Christian teachers in this matter is nowhere better expressed than in the Declaration on Religious Freedom of the recent Vatican Council:

> Therefore, this Vatican Synod urges everyone, especially those who are charged with the task of educating others, to do their utmost to form men who will respect the moral order and be obedient to lawful

authority. Let them form men too who will be lovers of true freedom
—men, in other words, who will come to decisions on their own judgment and in the light of truth, govern their activities with a sense of
responsibility, and strive after what is true and right, willing always to
join with others in cooperative effort.[5]

Bibliography

Abbott, Walter M., S.J., ed., *The Documents of Vatican II*, New York,
America Press, 1966.

D'Arcy, Eric, *Conscience and Its Right to Freedom*, New York, Sheed &
Ward, 1960.

Fagothey, Austin, *Right and Reason*, St. Louis, C. V. Mosby Co., 1959.

Haering, Bernard, C.SS.R., *The Law of Christ*, Westminster, Md., Newman Press, 1963, vol. I.

John XXIII, Pope, *Mater et magistra* and *Pacem in terris*, in *Seven Great
Encyclicals*, Glen Rock, N.J., Paulist Press, 1963.

McKenzie, John L., S.J., *Myths and Realities*, Milwaukee, Bruce Publishing Company, 1963.

Simon, Yves R., *A General Theory of Authority*, Notre Dame, Ind., University of Notre Dame Press, 1962.

Taylor, William L., "The Strategies of Protest," *Catholic Mind*, Septem-
ber, 1965.

[5] Declaration on Religious Freedom, p. 687, sec. 8.

*But the important thing is never to separate the visible
Church from the invisible Church. Let us not hover
over the clouds: to believe is to live. To live is to labor.
To labor is to be here and not there. Concretely to believe
the Church is to accept concretely to live within a church.*

KARL BARTH

REVEREND JOHN J. POWELL, S.J.

5   The Ecclesial Dimension of Faith

The Problem

The Church claims its origins in a small, unpretentious group of men, mostly fishermen, huddled loyally around a young Jewish rabbi most of whose teachings far outreached their understanding. The apostles knew all their theology in simple commitment to their Lord. Today the Church is a magnificent structure, rated second only to General Motors as the most efficient organization in the world. Its creed is a large but carefully refined and systematized catalogue of religious truths; its juridical system is very carefully codified in a lengthy book called the Code of Canon Law. The men who claim succession in office from the apostles under certain circumstances claim the prerogative of infallibility. A question very easily floats to the surface of the mind: is this highly elaborate organization really the Church of the Galilean fishermen? In addition to this perplexing question, the Church today is caught in crossfire between the conservative, who resents the slightest rubrical modification and moans for the good old days, and the liberal, who finds the air of the temple stale and commands the Church to break out of its medieval crust and become relevant to modern man. If a man is looking for an arena to work off his frustrations, he will certainly find something to attack in the Church, which is forever struggling with the agony of human weakness. It is, on this earth, a stumbling, battered pilgrim on its way to destiny and fulfillment in the promised land of the hereafter.

Criticism is safe only where there is love. It is shallow and immature to pick at another's limitations, real or imagined, unless one concedes all that is good in that other. There is obviously great need

47

48   REVEREND JOHN J. POWELL, S.J.

for free speech and public opinion in the *Ecclesia semper reformanda* (the Church always in renewal), but there is also the need of these credentials in the participants in the dialogue of renewal: recognition of the Church as God's magnificent means of redemption and the privileged site of encounter with God (the primordial sacrament), a love of the Church as such and a deep commitment to its best interests, and a competence in the areas under discussion. Today, I think, very many young voices rightfully seek a hearing in the dialogue of *aggiornamento*. Some have the sound of proper credentials, but very many seem to have the edge of personal indignation rather than love of the Church which is characterized by warmth and consideration. There is always this danger, and always the need to regard the total picture, to assess the good in balance with the bad, to offer constructive rather than destructive criticism in the Christian spirit, which is the spirit of compassion and kindness.

Too long we have asked, "*What* is the Church?" The question is, "*Who* is the Church?" I would like to take up both questions briefly. In so doing, I would like to emphasize that the full encounter with Christ is possible only in the Church.

On the Nature of Encounter

Enlisting the findings of human psychology, theologians today stress that man's way of knowing is "bodily," and that his encounter with Christ must somehow be bodily, that is, perceptible to the senses. If man were to give up his body, he would no longer be human, because his body is an integral part of him; it embodies him. Man's body incarnates him and manifests him to the world; it is his very mode of presence to the world. The body is the medium of all interpersonal relationships, and human life is both characterized and fulfilled by these relationships. Psychologists call it "intersubjectivity," and regard it as a given of human existence because it includes all the diverse ways of copresence that are possible to man. Humans are personally available to each other only because they are incarnate. It is through bodily expressions (words, gestures, facial expressions, signs) that our persons are manifested and that we are able to actualize or individuate (to use the term of depth psychology) our persons. The particular way each person expresses himself is called his personality. It is in the encounter of person with person that man experiences the most creative and rewarding moments of his life on this earth. It is such encounters that enable man to be more fully, to find his truest self.[1]

Man encountered God in the Old Testament in thunder and lightning over Sinai, in the burning bush, and in the face of the prophet; but God opens in the Incarnation a totally new dimension within the possibility of the divine-human encounter.

On the Nature of Faith

1. *Faith is the vital or living experience of encounter with God in His Son.* When God spoke His Word to man, in the Incarnation of His Son, in a sense God said all that He had to say to man. "In many fragmentary and varying utterances, God once spoke to our ancestors through the prophets; at the present time, in the final epoch of man, he has spoken to us through his Son, whom he has appointed heir of the universe" (Heb. 1:1-2). Because man is composed of body and soul, his natural way of knowing others initially and essentially involves his senses. He has to see and hear and touch. So we might say that, through the Incarnation, God has come to us in terms that we can understand. He has spoken our language. Saint John writes: "We proclaim what was from the beginning, what we have heard, what we have seen with our own eyes, what we have gazed upon, and what we have embraced with our own hands. I refer to the Word who is and who imparts life. . . . To you we proclaim what we have seen and heard, that you may share our treasure with us. That treasure is union with the Father and his Son, Jesus Christ" (1 Jn. 1-3).

Very often faith is defined as the acceptance of propositions or religious truths, and it is here that so many come to an impasse. Primarily it is the acceptance of Christ, the Word of God, in Whom and through Whom God says all that He would say to man. Very often faith is defined as an intellectual act, but the acceptance of a person is a response and experience far wider than the scope of intellect. It is a living experience that is totally enthralling, totally en-

---

[1] See Edward Schillebeeckx, "The Sacraments: An Encounter with God," in Daniel J. Callahan *et al.*, eds., *Christianity Divided: Protestant and Roman Catholic Theological Issues*, New York, Sheed & Ward, 1961. See also Remy Ewant, O.S.A., *Encounter*, Pittsburgh, Duquesne University Press, 1960; William A. Luijpen, O.S.A., *Existential Phenomenology*, Pittsburgh, Duquesne University Press, 1960, pp. 185 ff.; and Kenneth T. Gallagher, *The Philosophy of Gabriel Marcel*, New York, Fordham University Press, 1962, pp. 22 ff.

gaging; it challenges all the intellectual and emotional energies of man. It penetrates his mind, heart, and imagination. It is the encounter between our person and God's Person.

This was the insistence of Christ: believe *in Me*. He always required this acceptance of Himself in faith, whether it was by the father with his afflicted son, the blind man on the road to Jericho, or the ruler of the synagogue begging for his daughter's life. "Yes, it is my Father's will that everyone who looks upon the Son and believes in him shall have eternal life and be raised by me on the last day" (Jn. 6:44; see also Jn. 1:12, 1 Jn. 5:1, Acts 4:12, Mt. 11:27). Ultimately, Christian faith is in its Christ, the acceptance of a person, not simply a list of teachings. Christianity and the Church are rather a person than a doctrine. In His life upon this earth, it was on this personal adherence that Christ insisted; the fullness of His teachings would be given only with the coming of the Holy Spirit. Christ asks the apostles to be "witnesses of me" (Acts 1:8), and Paul tells the Corinthians that he has no other knowledge to offer them except the knowledge of Christ and Him crucified (1 Cor. 2:2). In fact, the subject of all apostolic preaching was the person of Christ—Peter speaking in Jerusalem (Acts 2:22-36) or to the household of Cornelius (Acts 10:34-43); Paul in Antioch of Pisidia (Acts 13:16-47), in Athens (Acts 17:22-31), in Corinth (1 Cor. 1:17-31). It was the same with John, writing his epistles in the twilight of his life (see 1 Jn. 1:1-8).

Fundamentally, then, it was *this living experience* that the apostles were charged to transmit. With the help of God (biblical inspiration), they tried to capture it in written records, and their writings (the New Testament) were both an expression of the Word God had spoken to man and the faith in which they accepted that Word. It is for this reason that the Gospels are called "confessional documents." But the frail vessel of words, the medium of written documents, could not hold all the meaning of this experience of and encounter with God in His Son. It was an experience that had to be relived, recaptured by all future generations of Christians. So it was transmitted through another channel, which we call sacred tradition, embracing the Christian liturgies and customs, the preaching, believing, and living witness of the Christian saints.

Therefore, above all, faith for a Christian is the Christian's personal acceptance of God in the person of His Son. "On God no man has ever laid his eyes; the only begotten Son, who rests in the Father's bosom, has himself been the interpreter" (Jn. 1:18). Accordingly, in *Pastoral Catechetics* we read, "Revelation is more than the unfolding of religious truth. It is God unveiling his personality under the impulse of intense love and coming into personal communion with man. Through the biblical, liturgical witness and doctrinal signs God comes to believers." [2]

2. *Faith, therefore, can never be understood unless it is lived.* The habit of faith or theological virtue is infused at baptism, and this habit is thought to facilitate the personal act of faith, which is made only after one has reached the age of reason. Each Christian must personally encounter and submit to Christ. Roger Troisfontaines, S.J., urges Christian theologians to begin not with lists of enunciated truths but "by experiencing it [the reality] as deeply as possible, by striving to grasp it in its concrete aspects so as only afterwards to pass on to objectification, to generalities and definitions." [3]

If the first thesis of this outline, which describes faith as an experience and way of life rather than as a disengaged act of a disengaged intellect, is found to be acceptable, then it is clear that no Christian can understand his faith unless he lives it. It would be an insipid denial for a Christian to reject a faith he has not really tried to put into practice. It would be equally insipid to reject a God he has not really strived to encounter. It is no easy matter to live one's Christian faith. The names of the virtues sound symphonically sweet; their practice is costly. There is fidelity in the encounter of the liturgy and sacraments, where contemporary man meets the contemporaneous Christ. There is the life of witness, which is a matter of always and everywhere. Each of us must say a personal *yes* or *no* to God and Christ; we must live out the I-Thou relationship that faith establishes, or run from it. The saddest thing would be to run from it without ever having tried to understand it, which means living it. But the more fully we live it the more we experience the reality of the encounter with God as a mystery of love.

Whatever is to be said about his orthodoxy, Père Teilhard de Chardin was a man of extraordinary faith. Two short excerpts from

---

[2] Johannes Hofinger, S.J., and Theodore Stone, eds., *Pastoral Catechetics*, New York, Herder and Herder, 1964; quoted in *Guide*, December, 1964, p. 12.
[3] Roger Troisfontaines, S.J., *Existentialism and Christian Thought*, London, Adam and Charles Black, 1949, p. 38.

his *Hymn of the Universe* reflect the nature of faith as a way of looking at things and a life to be led:

> I see and touch God everywhere. Everything means both everything and nothing to me. Everything is God to me; everything is dust to me.
>
> Yes, Lord God, I believe that . . . it is you that stand at the source of that impulse and at the end-point of that magnetic attraction to which all my life I must be docile, obedient to the initial impulse and eager to promote its developments. . . . It is not just your gifts that I discern; it is you yourself that I encounter, you who cause me to share in your own being, and whose hands mold me. . . . I encounter and I kiss your two wonderful hands . . . the organizing force of your Mystical Body.[4]

I would think that, in the case of the Christian who struggles with the act of faith without attempting the total engagement of the life of faith, there is at least an oblique relevance in the remark of Chesterton: "It isn't that Christianity has failed; it's just that no one has ever tried it."

3. *Faith is the gift of God; no man reasons his way into or out of faith.* The historical roots of Catholic apologetics, in the post-Reformation period, are traceable to a time of accelerated emotions and extravagant positions. Catholics seem to have lost sight of the *de fide* fact that only God can make a man a believer. No man can hear the Word of God and accept Him without a further gift from God. God has to enable man to hear His Word, and so He must sow the grace of faith in man's heart. God must open the ears of man if he is to hear and accept God's Word. We call this *the grace of faith*. In the last analysis, the truest answer to the question, "Why do you believe?" is that "God has given me the grace to do so."

In spite of misleading apologetics textbooks, faith is not the product of human reason compiling evidence. There is evidence for Catholic claims, of course, and this evidence yields the conclusion that the Catholic faith is reasonable or credible. It does not yield the conclusion: I believe. This is the work of grace.

Just as faith cannot be coerced by the muscular cogency of human argumentation, so is human argumentation ineffectual in attacking or denying faith. It is clearly sophomoric to say of faith, "I cannot

[4] Pierre Teilhard de Chardin, S.J., *Hymn of the Universe*, tr. Simon Bartholomew, New York, Harper & Row, Harper Torchbooks, 1965, pp. 84-85.

see it." No one can *see* it, in the sense of *understand* it. We can only accept it and, after having accepted it, live it.

In view of this presentation of faith as a vital encounter with God through His Son, an experience to be lived and a commitment out of the reach of human resources, one might ask if the heart of the problem hasn't actually been avoided. What about the *teachings* of the Church, which are the precise point of question for many young people struggling with faith? I do not think that this is the heart of the matter. The apostles themselves believed—and this remains always the central intuition of faith—in the person of Christ. They accepted all truth as revealed in Him, all truth was present to them in Him. All theological development is essentially a deepening of the understanding of this central intuition of faith: Christ. "But when he, the Spirit of truth, has come, he will lead you to the entire truth. . . . He is to glorify me, for he will draw upon what is mine and announce it to you" (see Jn. 16:7-15).

Before a Christian can deal competently with propositional truth, he must have a firm and deep faith in the person of Christ. Theology (on the amateur and professional levels) is, according to Anselm of Canterbury, *faith in search of understanding*. The light of faith is the light under which the believer must see all particularized truths. The experience of God in Christ must be deepened by the Holy Spirit first; and then (and only then) there arises in the Christian believer "a sense of Christ," a taste and judgment in the things of God, a deeper perception of God's truth, and an increased understanding of God's ways and dispositions which very often undercut our own human ways and dispositions. This is what theologians call *Christian connaturality*. It is not natural since it is the work of grace, and yet it is like a natural instinct or intuition. Since it results in the Christian from the fullness of the divine indwelling and the impulses of grace, no amount of dialectical or analytical facility, which is a purely human endowment, can provide this connatural instinct. Christian connaturality can be deepened only through a deepened union with God in Christ, which is the life of faith. Only the Christian who is committed in faith has the proper light and perspective for the search of understanding. He will have to make the complete gift of himself in faith before he will receive the rewards of understanding.

Many young people who are struggling with faith seem to be psychologically unable or unwilling to make the total gift of their person to another person, either divine or human. Insecure (and immature) in the possession of their own person, they find the surrender of faith frightening. Like most people, they imagine that God can be satisfied if they merely give Him things (worship, service, obedience) in exchange for salvation. They bargain with God, and religion becomes a *quid pro quo* business deal such as it was with the Pharisees in the time of Christ. They are unwilling or unable to see that God is satisfied only with the gift of the total person through the direct, free, and total commitment of faith. The issues raised as rebuttals of faith are decoys. The essential problem is the personal encounter with God in Christ.

When our Lord had confronted His Jewish following with the truth of the eucharist—"unless you eat my body and drink my blood" —they found "such language hard to bear." He asked them, "Does this make you waver in your faith?" And he diagnoses the heart of the problem: "The trouble is that there are some among you that have no faith." It was the hour of decision, and Saint John tells us that "thereupon many of his disciples went back to their old life and would no longer associate with him." So Christ turned to the twelve, and asked if they, too, were going to leave him. It was Peter who spoke up: "Lord, to whom shall we go? You have the message of eternal life; we firmly believe and are fully convinced that you are the Holy One of God!" (see Jn. 6). They would only later understand the truth of His body and blood, but they had made the basic commitment to His person, which is the act of faith. If we leave You, to Whom shall we go?

The Encounter with God in the Contemporary World

God has uttered His Word, the Word made flesh. But this was some two thousand years ago, and the modern world is not precisely contemporary with this intrusion of God into human history. The problem is that Christ is now ascended into heaven; He is not my contemporary. I cannot touch and see and hear (encounter) Him as Saint John and the apostles once did. My personal faith must somehow be radicated in my own earthly condition of existence, in my present bodily existence with all its wondrous unwieldiness. It points up the seemingly absurd element in Christian faith: to affirm that man, in this bodily state, can encounter a wholly other God. Yet for man, to believe, just as to be, is to believe in a body. It is only the presence of the Church that allows this possibility.

Father Karl Rahner summarizes his argument for calling the Church the "primal and fundamental sacrament" as follows:

> The Church is the official presence of the grace of Christ in the public history of the one human race. In its socially organized form the People of God as in fact redeemed by Christ receives his permanent presence throughout history. And when we come to examine what this one reality implies, it means a presence, as it were an incarnation, of the truth of Christ in the Church through Scripture, tradition, and the magisterium; a similar embodiment and presence of Christ's will in the Church's teaching when it announces Christ's precepts in her pastoral office and her constitution; and a presence and embodiment, again analogous to the Incarnation, of the grace of Christ, for the individual as such, through the sacraments. Viewed in relation to the Christ, the Church is the abiding promulgation of his grace-giving presence in the world. Viewed in relation to the sacraments, the Church is the primal and fundamental sacrament.[5]

So Christ founded a structured Church which would sacramentally (the sign of His presence and grace) extend Him in time till the end of time and in space to the ends of the world. He has established this Church as a site of encounter, where He is perennially present and available: He acts and sanctifies in the sacraments, He teaches through the Magisterium, He offers sacrifice in the mass. But all encounter involves mutual availability and openness. And so man must approach this sacramental encounter with Christ with the fullest openness to Christ's activity. It is an encounter that requires preparation and subsequent reflection. Father Schillebeeckx writes:

> The Sacraments bring about the encounter with Christ in exactly those seven instances in which, on account of the demands of a special situation of Christian life, a man experiences a special and urgent need of communion with him. They are the divine act of redemption itself, manifest in the sacred environment of the living Church, making a concrete appeal to man and taking hold of him in a living way, as really as does the embrace of a mother for her child. And it is not enough for the child merely to know that its mother loves it; it needs the actual embrace to perfect the experience of love.[6]

Consequently, if faith is really a living encounter with God in His Son, belief in the Church is not an additional truth I must accept but the very condition, *sine qua non*, of the full encounter that we

[5] Karl Rahner, S.J., *The Church and the Sacraments*, New York, Herder and Herder, 1963, p. 19; see pp. 9-24.
[6] Edward Schillebeeckx, *The Sacrament of the Encounter with God*, New York, Sheed & Ward, 1963, p. 199.

call faith. In the end it is this Church, the bride and body and presence of Christ in the world today, that is the avenue by which man
goes to the encounter with God, and in which he is met by God. It
is, in Kierkegaard's phrase, the "absolute paradox."

When a person, infant or adult, is brought to the threshold of the
Church for the rite of baptism, which incorporates him into the body
of Christ, he is asked: "[Name,] what do you ask of the Church of
God?" The response is: "Faith." If faith is viewed as the living experience or encounter with God in His Son, then it is only this
Church, the Sacrament of Christ's presence and grace, that can give
him the faith he seeks.

If a person finds himself unable to accept this identification of
Christ and His Church, he will certainly never understand the thun-
dering question of Christ to a man named Saul, whose chief preoc-
cupation at the time was to destroy the Church: "Saul, Saul, why do
you persecute *me?*" (Acts 9:4).

The Church Is "the People of God" and "the Body of Christ"

The essential point is that we cannot really encounter God in
Christ unless the person and saving acts of Christ are somehow present to us in a bodily way here and now. This is precisely the function of the Church. The presence of God in Palestine, under the sign
of an assumed human nature, is now present under the veil of sacramental, liturgical, biblical, and magisterial signs; and what God did
in Palestine two thousand years ago under the veil of historical hap-
penings is now present to us under these signs. It is in and through
the person of Christ, present in the Church, that He acts on me and
I open to Him; He is present to me and I am present to Him. This is
what is meant by encounter.

In treating the ecclesial dimension of faith, we must not overlook
the fact that men do not encounter God as isolated individuals, nor
does God save men as individuals. God not only saves us through
Christ, but we must save one another because Christ has so willed it.
He entrusts the distribution of His graces to the members of His
Church. It is the reality of the *total* or *whole* Christ. There is no authentic Christian act or life of faith that does not include perception
of this reality. It has been said that there are two ways to deny Christ
or fail in faith: in Himself and in His members. Dorothy Day once
publicly wondered which was the more blasphemous denial.

Much has been written and said on this subject. The epistles of Saint Paul are surfeited with the reality, chiefly under the biblical image of the body of Christ. The Fathers of the Church clearly reflect the reality under the headings "body of Christ" [7] and "people of God." [8] There have been many papal encyclicals on this unity of Christians in Christ, culminated by Pope Pius XII's *Mystici Corporis*. The Constitution on the Church of Vatican II devotes a whole chapter, 2, to the unity of the people of God; section 9 reads: "God, however, does not make men holy and save them merely as individuals, without bond or link between one another. Rather has it pleased Him to bring men together as one people. . . ." There has also been a spate of excellent books and articles, at almost every level of presentation. [9]

If the authentic act and life of faith must embrace this reality of the people of God and the total Christ, again one might wonder whether this truth is placed squarely before Christian believers. I think that what has been said of faith earlier in this paper must be said of the ecclesial dimension of faith: it cannot be understood *unless it is lived*. I would submit that this is the core of the problem of faith. Those who experience the sharpest agonies usually experience them at a safe distance from the exercise of faith. I would further submit that this is the danger of irrelevance feared by those who are teaching theology.

Conclusion

A recent survey on religion in the United States revealed that a very high percentage (94 percent) of Americans think of themselves as religious and endowed with faith. The same survey also illustrated that this faith professed by so many has only a negligible effect on their lives. It is a painfully clear demonstration of the irrelevance of faith. Actually, it is the death of faith, because the one thing authentic faith cannot be is irrelevant.

[7] See Ernest Mura, R.S.V., *The Nature of the Mystical Body*, St. Louis, B. Herder Book Co., 1963.
[8] See the essays by Congar, Schnackenburg, and Dupont in *The Church and Mankind*, vol. I of the *Concilium* series, Glen Rock, N.J., Paulist Press, 1965.
[9] See, for example, Emile Mersch, *The Whole Christ*, Milwaukee, Bruce Publishing Co., 1938; Paul Furfey, *Fire on the Earth*, New York, Macmillan Company, 1936; John Murphy, *The Living Christ*, Milwaukee, Bruce Publishing Co., 1952; and André de Bouis, *What Is the Church?*, tr. R. F. Treuett, New York, Hawthorn Books, 1961.

From the viewpoint of the theology teacher, struggling with students who are struggling with faith, I think that the general approach is far too academic, noetic, apologetic. Most people are not intellectual, and most decisions are not made on intellectual grounds. The great Cardinal Newman wrote in his *Grammar of Assent:* "The heart is commonly reached, not through reason, but through the imagination, by means of direct impressions, by the testimony of facts and events, by history, by description. Persons influence us, voices melt us, looks subdue us, deeds inflame us." [10]

Faith is obviously initiated by God, but man is free to respond or not. He will go to the encounter of faith or he will not. If he goes, he will experience the presence and power of God, and all the well-rehearsed arguments made in favor of faith will most likely seem superfluous.

---

[10] John Henry Cardinal Newman, *Grammar of Assent,* London, Longmans, Green, 1891, pp. 92-93.

Respect for the word *is the first commandment in the discipline by which a man can be educated to maturity—intellectual, emotional and moral.*

DAG HAMMARSKJOLD

SISTER RODERICK O'NEIL, R.S.H.M.

6   Hermeneutics:
The Encompassing-Which-Scripture-Is

Recently I visited the Turner exhibition at New York's Museum of Modern Art. The display was aptly entitled "Imagination and Reality." The more I experienced the art of this precursor of abstract expressionism, the more relevant it became to the subject of this paper. Only in retrospect did I discover why. One art critic described Turner's imagination in terms very akin to the new direction in hermeneutics: "His imagination was his capacity to brush aside the trivia that assume disproportionate importance in daily life because we are close to them, and to think of the universe in terms of a manifestation of powers. . . ." [1]

So with the science of interpretation, that is, hermeneutics. It invites us to think of Scripture in terms of a personal revelation (that is, a manifestation of persons). The exegetical trivia that assumed a disproportionate importance in the latter half of the nineteenth and early twentieth centuries are officially dismissed in Vatican II's Dogmatic Constitution on Divine Revelation.

The effect of the Constitution in regard to hermeneutics is somewhat like that of LSD on human consciousness. The supersonic crack is perhaps only audible to the sensitized ears of the exegete. From an apodictic position on the inerrancy of Scripture, the Church's doctrine has become richly positive, centering as it does on salvific truth.[2] The criterion in judging the inspired nature of Scripture is "saving truth."

---

[1] John Canaday, "Latching On to Turner," *The New York Times*, March 27, 1966, p. X-29.

[2] Barnabas M. Ahern, C.P., "Scriptural Aspects of the Constitution on Divine Revelation," Notre Dame Conference on Theological Issues of Vatican II, March 21, 1966.

The notion of inerrancy had so dominated the older manual treatment of inspiration that hermeneutics became "the art of saving the Bible from error." [3] "Saving truth" expands the scope of this science to the degree that in time hermeneutics could subsume the whole of theology. Carroll Stuhlmueller, C.P., has defined salvation as "the exhilarating knowledge of God's love." Salvific truth is personal, then. With such a personal focus, a previously negative and almost nervous art of saving the Bible from error has become the art of saving the Christian from a dull, drab interpretation of Scripture.

But lest our optimistic prism distort the hermeneutical picture, we must consider the stormy reality that confronts this science of interpretation. Here, too, the analogy with Turner's art is significant. The cataclysms of cosmic elements—fire, earth, air, and water—that constituted reality for this nineteenth-century artistic genius have a cataclysmic counterpart in the elements of language, culture, distance, and time that vibrate in the written word of Scripture.

Luis Alonso Schökel has outlined these elements well in his article "Hermeneutics in the Light of Language and Literature." He describes how language itself is triply interpretive, "first as the human faculty of speech, secondly, as a concrete language and thirdly in its personal use." [4] The interpretive operation that is involved in understanding is so complex that after studying its several steps one ceases to be hurt at occasional misunderstandings, and is simply lost in wonder before the miracle of ever being understood.

Take the speaker's objectivized experience and the listener's consequent act of subjectification, spice with temperamental differences as exist between the meticulous, receptive listener and the more playful, apperceptive speaker, and you have a colorful picture of a highly complex hermeneutic process! The hermeneutic problem sets in when there is a difference of language, not to mention distance. The problem is compounded when the language is literary, that is, more prone to concentrated matter and refined form. This is why a knowledge of the literary forms employed by the biblical authors is indispensable to any interpreter of Scripture. Literary forms are the vehicles used to communicate religious fact and experience.

Father Schökel considers one of the most vexing hermeneutic

[3] Luis Alonso Schökel, S.J., *The Inspired Word*, New York, Herder and Herder, 1965, p. 309.
[4] Luis Alonso Schökel, S.J., "Hermeneutics in the Light of Language and Literature," *Catholic Biblical Quarterly*, July, 1963, p. 375.

problems of our times to be that of transposing the Bible's literary language into the technical language of theology. The problem has been with us since Nicaea, and is rendered more acute, contends Father Schökel, by the gap between some recent scholastic theologians and Scripture. Karl Rahner's attempt to transpose the technical language of theology into more personalist categories, so dear to existential man, seems to be narrowing that gap. He has written well that dogmatic theology uprooted from Scripture is sterile. Apart from the vibrant warmth of God's inspired word, doctrine is chilling to man's body-person.

Interestingly, depending upon your philosophic stance, language is a threat or a thrust to revelation, opaque or diaphanous with "saving truth." Karl Jaspers sees the attempt to objectify any experience of transcendence in the form of a literary production as debasing the very notion of divinity. He maintains that "When biblical religions arose, a genuine revelation-consciousness was still possible. But today, because of a more perfect consciousness, any claim for divine revelation is utter illusion." [5] This idea is reminiscent of Freud's thesis in *The Future of an Illusion*, that religion is an escape mechanism by which reality becomes tolerable.[6] Far from an illusory means, Carl Jung sees it as being in the nature of man that he depend upon the medium of religion in his confrontation with the more shattering aspect of reality which is God.

Taking the philosophic posture of the later Heidegger, the post-Bultmannians (or Marburgers, as Bultmann's former students are sometimes called) view language as appreciatively as Jung regards religion. Considering man to be by nature religious, they see reality as linguistic and language as man's glory. *Language orchestrates the shattering truth that is the silent voice of being!* In the later Heideggerian philosophy, "Being calls upon man; it forces thought upon man, and this calls forth language. It is not so much that man consciously seeks words as signs to express himself or his experience. The silent voice of being speaks through man in language. Language uses man." [7]

[5] Paul Hossfield, "Karl Jaspers and Religion," *Philosophy Today*, Winter, 1959, p. 278.
[6] See Sigmund Freud, *The Future of an Illusion*, Garden City, Doubleday & Company, 1964, Chap. VIII.
[7] Raymond E. Brown, S.S., "After Bultmann, What?", *Catholic Biblical Quarterly*, January, 1964, p. 17.

The hermeneutic of the later Heidegger is far from—or beyond—that classical science taken up with the rules for interpreting Scripture, three traditional divisions of which are noematics, heuristics, and prophoristics. The new hermeneutic encompasses the whole dynamic process of God speaking to man. It is not so much concerned with interpretation. The word communicates understanding, without any technological assistance. This might come as a disappointment to the school of social analysts who herald the day when through technology man will be in an immediate relationship with everybody and everything. Marshall McLuhan, the outstanding voice in this school, has recently published a book which sounds as if we're in for "instant understanding."

In the hermeneutic of the post-Bultmannian, all that stands between man and the message is the static of self. As the doctrine of God's word, ". . . it allows the word of God to speak to us." [8] What for Bultmann was the hermeneutical presupposition has become for the post-Bultmannian hermeneutic a goal. This is because in the latter the text interprets us. The self-understanding that Bultmann presupposed in approaching Scripture is found by his former disciples only in the text. And here we seem to experience a real flip-flop in the post-Bultmannian perspective, mainly because language is so closely related to the theological enterprise. "The problem seems to be less of demythologizing language so that Scripture is 'brought up' to modern man and more of criticizing modern man with his distorted relationship to himself so that he is 'brought back' to Scripture." [9]

Here is an interesting variation in movement, compared with the centripetal movement of the existential interpreter and the centrifugal movement of the more scientific interpreter. Jaspers' concern that our approach to transcendence be ever new and fluid might be gratified by such hermeneutic vigor. Indeed, the terminology is so fluid that some could regard it as a conspiracy.[10]

Nevertheless, no such suspicion will intimidate the academic consciousness that surrounds this scriptural force field. The student's psyche is in process. Its tolerance of ambiguity is greater than before the physicist Niels Bohr proposed the principle of complementarity

[8] Ibid., p. 19.
[9] Ibid., pp. 19-20.
[10] P. Joseph Cahill, "Rudolf Bultmann and Post-Bultmann Tendencies," Catholic Biblical Quarterly, April, 1964, p. 158.

whereby two theories are held valid in explaining the nature of matter, even though they are mutually exclusive when applied simultaneously. In the light of this principle, the student is less scandalized by the apparent contradictions in Scripture. Bergson's flow of intuition disposes the student to the inner reality of things. Historically his concern is with the "inside" of events rather than with a clinical analysis of data. The synoptic problem is a pseudo-problem for the budding existentialist, who is so enamored of subjectivity that he would protest if the synoptics *had* come up with the same picture of Christ!

So the circle of consciousness is growing in proportion to the hermeneutical circle. And that Spirit who is ever active in the inner- and outermost limits of our being is enjoying a second Pentecost. His activity should give heart to the shakiest student of his inspired word.

If understanding of revelation is to grow, the philosopher, the speculative theologian, and the professional exegete must work together. Communication is a real problem in this age of specialization. Depending upon the attitude of the teacher of sacred doctrine, the proliferation of specialized branches of knowledge will be cause for either celebration or alarm. If he appreciates his times and is impressionable enough to yield to the truth in them, he himself will be the hermeneutical key that will open to students the unfathomable riches that await them in Scripture.

A sociopolitically variegated key can unlock the revelation latent in the *Denver Daily News* or the *New York Times*. Soon the student's sense of interpretation will find salvific meaning—that is, a potentiality for redemptive consequences—in the turmoil of a Selma or a Saigon. Rather than retreat from the political and social crises of his time into the world of eschatological issues, a native habitat of the intellectual, he will find in these very crises construction material for the eschatological kingdom. Through experience in scriptural interpretation, the student will be that much more responsive to the gospel-of-everyday that summons him to "imaginative urbanity and mature secularity." [11]

[11] Harvey Cox, *The Secular City*, New York, Macmillan Company, 1965, p. 83.

For what is the church save the assembly of people before God, or the movement of those who, abandoning all relative and finite goals, turn toward the infinite end of life? It is the ecclesia *which has been called out of the pluralism and the temporalism of the world to the supreme reality and only good, on which the goodness of all finite things depends.*

HELMUT RICHARD NIEBUHR

SISTER MARY ANTHONY WAGNER, O.S.B.

7 The Christian Assembly

It has become evident to all of us that the Constitution on the Sacred Liturgy is one of the great documents of the Second Vatican Council. However, since it is a matter not so much of legislation to be implemented from above as of an exposition of the faith to be examined by us on the level of faith, its importance will not be realized or its intent be effective without deep and productive study on our part. Though the Constitution has juridical aspects, its regulations for the acts of worship are founded on great realities of *being* within the Christian community. Thus, while the Constitution is not styled as dogmatic, theological concepts underlie all its discussions. Piet Fransen designates two of the more important of these as (1) a conception of the Church, not as a pyramid structure of hierarchical powers juridically interrelated, but as the faithful consecrated by baptism and confirmation and gathered together into the people of God, whose internal cohesion is assured by the presence and sanctifying indwelling of the Trinity; and (2) a view of the sacraments, not as certain automatic signs to be employed for salvation, but as contacts with Christ which demand a personal response of the Christian.[1] Here we have not only a dynamic approach to the liturgy but also to a new theology of the Church.

This paper will deal in part with the concept of the Church. More specifically, I shall treat of the reality of the Christian assembly as described in its prelude in the *Qehal Yahweh* of the Old Testament, in its fulfillment in the new Israel of the New Testament, and in the

---

[1] Piet Fransen, S.J., "Theological Implications of Liturgical Discussion at the Council," in Hugo Rahner *et al., The Church: Readings in Theology,* New York, P. J. Kenedy & Sons, 1963, pp. 171-193.

unfolding and exercise of this holy congregation in the period of the apostolic Fathers.[2]

Perhaps we will do best not to define or describe the people of God as such but to allow the full reality to grow in our loving understanding as we review God's dealings with His people in the past. We may then be able to make the transfer to ourselves today as the new people of God, for whom vital insights into what we are and do when we gather for liturgy have been provided in the Constitutions on the Sacred Liturgy and on the Church.

In the Old Testament

Yahweh's holy people (*Qehal Yahweh*) came into existence on that day of covenant on Mount Sinai (Ex. 19), later to be known simply as the "day of the assembly" (Dt. 9:10), when Yahweh called His people together through His elected servant Moses, purifying them and readying them (Ex. 19:10-14) to hear and receive His law, and to worship Yahweh Who was covenanting with them (Ex. 19:5-6). The very word for assembly—*ekklesia*, derived from *kaleo*, to call, and *ex*, out—signifies this convocation by God. Thus, the *ekklesia Dei* became the property of Yahweh. In and during the congregation God appeared, was present (Ex. 19:18-20). God's help, graciously bestowed on His people, evoked from them thanksgiving, praise, and sacrifices, which in turn caused the coming of Yahweh again in benediction upon His people. Thus the assembly concluded with a meal in the presence of Yahweh (Ex. 24:9-11).

These fundamental elements, of being called, responding, and being sanctified, were present in every renewal of the covenant between Yahweh and His holy people: at the consecration of the holy tent (Lv. 9:23-24), at the renewal under King Josiah (2 Chr. 23:1-3, 21-25), and finally at the renewal after the captivity (Neh. 8:1-9, 39). Each celebration was a recalling (an *anamnesis*) of the deeds of Yahweh, a renewal of the covenant at which the present assembly reactualized the event of Sinai, a renewal at which a younger gener-

---

[2] I am indebted for both inspiration and information to a fellow faculty member of the summer session of the Graduate Program in Sacred Doctrine at Saint John's University, Collegeville, Minnesota: Dom Suitbert Benz, O.S.B., of Maria Laach Abbey, Germany, who taught a course on the Christian assembly. His article "The Monastery as a Christian Assembly" appeared in the June, 1966, issue of *The American Benedictine Review*.

ation now became God's people, the *Qehal Yahweh*[3] (Dt. 5:1-5; 29:1-2). Hear the words of Moses: "The Lord our God made a covenant with us at Horeb; it was not with our forefathers that the Lord made this covenant, but with ourselves, with those of us who are all here alive today" (Dt. 5:2-3). The *hodie* of the liturgical celebration is evident.

All the gatherings for the annual celebrations of the saving deeds of Yahweh (at the Passover, at Pentecost, and at the Feast of Tabernacles) were also a real perpetuation, a re-enacting of God's helping presence in the midst of His people (Ex. 12:14, 17, 27; 16:16-17). To exclude oneself from the celebration meant to be cut off from God's people (Nm. 9:13). So it was that each of these celebrations had a threefold dimension: (1) a commemoration of God's saving deeds of the past, effective once and forever; (2) a representation now of that salvation, resulting from those saving deeds; and (3) an anticipating outlook to a future possession of salvation. Especially after the Babylonian captivity, these celebrations had a strong eschatological tone: a looking for the Messiah with a new and everlasting covenant (Is. 61:8), a time when Yahweh would appear again, when a new Israel would again be His holy people, "the redeemed of the Lord" (Is. 62:12), with a new heart and a new spirit (Ez. 18:31).

The Assembly of the Liturgy

The Constitution on the Sacred Liturgy says that "The wonderful works of God among the people of the Old Testament were but a prelude to the work of Christ the Lord in redeeming mankind and giving perfect glory to God," and that "He achieved this task principally by the paschal mystery of his blessed passion, resurrection from the dead, and glorious ascension. . . . For it was from the side of Christ as he slept the sleep of death upon the cross that there came forth 'the wondrous sacrament of the whole Church' "[4] (Const. sec. 5).[5] At an annual and final celebration of the Passover of the Mount

[3] The people assembled by Yahweh (*Qehal Yahweh*) is an important notion of the Old Testament. The Septuagint uses *ekklesia* one hundred times when the corresponding Hebrew is *Qahal*. The term *laos* is used two thousand times to designate the Israelites as God's holy people in opposition to the nonpeople, the *ethnoi* (pagans).
[4] See the prayer before the second lesson for Holy Saturday, as it was in the Roman Missal before the restoration of Holy Week.
[5] *The Constitution on the Sacred Liturgy of the Second Vatican Council and the Motu Proprio of Pope Paul VI* (Const.), with a commentary by Gerard S. Sloyan, Glen Rock, N.J., Paulist Press, 1964, sec. 5.

Sinai covenant, a new people of God is called, is born, is manifested to the world. A new temple of God stands erected upon Calvary's hill, in which the new people of God will perpetually celebrate their worship and their dedication to Him Whom they can now call "Abba, Father." And as Christ was sent by the Father, so also He sent the apostles, filled with the Holy Spirit (Const. sec. 6), to proclaim His death and resurrection victory (Mk. 16:14), to plunge (baptize) men into His paschal mystery (Rom. 6:4), and to proclaim His death until He comes (1 Cor. 11:26).

"To come together" (ekklesia) is also the real vocation of the new people of God (Const. sec. 12). Now the holy people of God is gathered around Christ being present in their midst, continuing the work of salvation which He began in His passion and resurrection. The key sentence in the entire Constitution appears in section 7: "To accomplish so great a work, Christ is always present." [6] If we do not admit this full presence of Christ in His Church, we are finished with liturgy; we are overlooking the theology of liturgy, of the priesthood. With Christ acting in its midst, the new people of God is called "to come together" (Const. sec. 10). This Christian convocation, this coming together with Christ in its midst both in word and in deed (Const. sec. 6; Lk. 24:27), is the summit toward which the activity of the Church is directed and the font from which her power flows (Const. sec. 10); the aim of apostolic works is that all who are made sons of God should come together to praise Him in the midst of His Church (Const. sec. 10).

According to the Constitution on the Sacred Liturgy, the Christian assembly is the gathering of all the faithful, each of whom "is called to pray with his brethren" (Const. sec. 12) and by reason of his baptism has the "right and duty" (sec. 14) of active participation in the liturgical celebration, which "by its very nature" (sec. 14) requires the collaboration of the whole body of Christ. The liturgical celebration is the actual and concrete assembly (secs. 7, 26) in whose midst Christ is ever acting, associating the Church with Himself in this great work wherein God is perfectly glorified and men are sanc-

---

[6] In an oral commentary I heard by Father Herman Schmidt, S.J., a peritus at the Vatican Council and a member of the Liturgical Commission, on the Constitution on the Sacred Liturgy, he stressed how the use of praesens adest, used instead of praesens est, puts emphasis upon the personal presence of Christ here and now.

tified (sec. 7). It is the "pre-eminent manifestation of the Church" (sec. 41), a manifestation of "the mystery of Christ and the real nature of the true Church . . . to those who are outside as a sign lifted up among the nations under which the scattered children of God may be gathered together" (sec. 2). Therefore, this Christian assembly is the very expression of the Church as a worshiping community, in the midst of which God dwells and in which the faithful have access to Christ by Whom they are constantly being made into the holy people of God.

Thus it is that the active participation of the faithful in liturgical celebrations is the primary principle of all liturgical reforms (Const. sec. 79). Active participation is "the primary and indispensable source from which the faithful are to derive the true Christian spirit" (sec. 14), the Christian life, the call to the new people of God. Thus, too, it is evident that liturgical celebration and not doctrine is the essence of Christian life. To the faithful, then, belongs not merely *a* part in the celebration but *their* part (secs. 2, 21).

In the New Testament

Looking into the New Testament, we find the disciples frequently called together: in the assembly for the paschal meal at the last supper; on Easter Sunday and its octave, when Christ appeared in their midst (Jn. 20:19, 26); at the Ascension (Acts 1:4), for which reason they expected Christ's return among them; at their return to the city where they waited, "devoting themselves with one mind to prayer" (Acts 1:13-14); at the election of Matthias, "one who has been associated with us . . . to join us as witness to his resurrection" (Acts 1:15-26); at Pentecost, when they "were meeting together" (Acts 2:1), waiting for the power from on high, and when Peter announced repentance to the universal assembly gathered at this first manifestation of the new Israel, to all those "whom the Lord our God calls to him" (Acts 2:38-39). To that early Christian community "every day the Lord added people who were saved" (Acts 2:47), who received the word of God through the apostles (Acts 2:42). The assembly of believers, that is, the baptized (Acts 2:44), responded to this teaching with the "breaking of bread and prayers" (Acts 2:42); and their daily life of charity was consequent upon their cultic gathering (Acts 2:45).

In the New Testament, *ekklesia* is used often to designate the Christian congregation (Acts 2:47; 5:11; 15:41; 16:5; 1 Cor. 1:2; 11:16), as well as for different assemblies, at Jerusalem, Antioch, and so forth (Acts 11:22, 26; 12:1, 5; 15:4, 22). The *ekklesia* is where an assembly exists; it is not the composition of many local assemblies; it applies to both Jewish and Gentile Christians (Acts 20:28; 1 Cor. 14:4); it is not quantity but quality which determines the body, which is the gathering by God of those who belong to Him (Acts 2:38-42; Mt. 18-20) by faith and baptism. The early Christian community was aware of being the new *Qehal Yahweh* (Acts 15:14; 18:10; Rom. 9:25; 2 Cor. 6:16; Tit. 2:14, 1 Pet. 2:9-10; Heb. 4:9; 8:10; 13:12; Ap. 18:4; 21:3). Christ's assembly is the true people of God (Rom. 9:6; 1 Cor. 10:18; Gal. 6:16) even though it is composed of Gentiles (Acts 15:14; Gal. 3:26 ff.; 1 Cor. 12:2-3; Col. 3:11); it is the seed of Abraham (Gal. 3:29); it is the true circumcision (Phil. 3:3); it is the temple of God (1 Cor. 3:16). This is the *ekklesia* in the midst of which God dwells, and it has access to Him, because it has been sanctified by the blood of the new covenant.

In the First Christian Centuries

In the writings of the apostolic Fathers of the Church, we also have frequent reference to what it means for God's people to have been called together by God and sanctified by Him:[7] "the assembly . . . elect and worthy of God,"[8] "the holy and universal assembly in every place,"[9] the Church "to be gathered from the four winds,"[10] indicative of the Church at the end of time. The people are exhorted "to assemble more frequently to render thanks and praise to God."[11] A gathering for the celebration of the eucharist is the deepest expression of the community as a congregating of those who have the same faith: "Come together in common, one and all without exception in

[7] St. Clement of Rome, "The Letter to the Corinthians," tr. Francis X. Glimm, in *The Apostolic Fathers*, New York, Cima Publishing Co., 1947, Introduction.

[8] St. Ignatius of Antioch, "The Letter to the Trallians," tr. Gerald G. Walsh, S.J., in *ibid.*, Introduction.

[9] "The Martyrdom of St. Polycarp," tr. Francis Glimm, in *ibid.*, Introduction.

[10] "The Didache or Teaching of the Twelve Apostles," tr. Francis X. Glimm, in *ibid.*, 10, 5.

[11] St. Ignatius of Antioch, "The Letter to the Ephesians," tr. Gerald G. Walsh, S.J., in *ibid.*, 13, 1.

charity, in one faith and in one Jesus Christ," [12] an idea which later explained the axiom *lex orandi, lex credendi.*

The assemblies are to be on the Lord's day, "on which through Him and through His death, our life arose." [13] The coming together is to be not only in one place but also "in concord";[14] not a mere social gathering, but "one Eucharist" because of "one flesh of our Lord, Jesus Christ, and one chalice . . . one altar . . . one bishop." [15] The singing, a sign of the people's concord, is "one voice through Jesus Christ to the Father," [16] a unanimity founded in obedience to the bishop,[17] and rendering the prayers of the whole stronger than that of a single man.[18] Only in the assembly do the harmonies of faith and worship find their true expression: ". . . let there be in common a single prayer, one petition, one mind, one hope, in love, in the unmixed joy which is Jesus Christ, who is the best of all. Hasten all of you together as to one temple of God, to one altar, to Jesus Christ alone, who came from one Father in whom He is and to whom He has returned." [19] Membership in the Christian body is achieved through faith and baptism, by which we become the sons of God.[20] The preparation and the celebration for baptism are acts of the assembly;[21] the baptized are brought "to the place where are assembled those whom we call brethren, to offer up sincere prayers in common for ourselves, for the baptized person, and for all other persons." [22]

The assembly is the sign of unity; those who "abstain from the Eucharist and prayer" [23] separate themselves from the assembly.[24] It is not a mass of individuals but a well-ordered and hierarchically

[12] *Ibid.,* 20, 1-2.
[13] St. Ignatius of Antioch, "The Letter to the Magnesians," tr. Gerald G. Walsh, S.J., in *ibid.,* 9, 1; "The Didache," 14, 1; and St. Justin Martyr, "The First Apology," tr. Thomas Falls, in *The Apostolic Fathers,* New York, Christian Heritage, 1948, 67.
[14] St. Clement of Rome, *op. cit.,* 34, 6-7.
[15] St. Ignatius of Antioch, "The Letter to the Philadelphians," tr. Gerald G. Walsh, S.J., in *The Apostolic Fathers,* Cima, 4.
[16] St. Ignatius of Antioch, "The Letter to the Ephesians," 4.
[17] St. Ignatius of Antioch. "The Letter to the Magnesians," 6.
[18] St. Ignatius of Antioch, "The Letter to the Ephesians," 5.
[19] St. Ignatius of Antioch, "The Letter to the Magnesians," 7.
[20] "The Didache," 9, 5; and St. Justin Martyr, *op. cit.,* 66, 1.
[21] "The Didache," 7, 4.
[22] St. Justin Martyr, *op. cit.,* 65.
[23] St. Ignatius of Antioch, "The Letter to the Smyrnaeans," tr. Gerald G. Walsh, S.J., in *The Apostolic Fathers,* Cima, 6-7.
[24] St. Ignatius of Antioch, "The Letter to the Ephesians," 5.

structured body[25] expressing itself in a unity but variety of func-
tions.[26] The liturgical gathering is essentially connected with the
hierarchical position of the bishop. It seems to be his noblest and
most important task to preside over the assemblies for the celebration
of the eucharist or baptism or other communal exercises: "Wherever
the bishop appears, there let the people be; as wherever Jesus Christ
is, there is the Catholic Church." [27] The Christian assembly is not
identical with the bishop, however; it includes the presbytery, the
deacons, and the laymen,[28] the laymen choosing the bishops[29] and
the deacons being for the service of the people.[30] The brethren who
come together in one faith form one great family in which the
bishop, though having special powers of saying the eucharistic prayers and of explaining the holy Scriptures, has them in a function of
service for the assembly; dialogue between the bishop and the people
at the eucharistic celebration has been an essential part since the beginning.[31]

All of this is not only clear but emphatic, therefore, in such writers
as the author of *The Didache*, Saint Ignatius of Antioch, Saint Justin
Martyr, and Saint Clement of Rome. For Tertullian, too, the assembly is the real expression of the Christian life; the gathering for the
celebration is identical with the Church.[32] It is also clear in *The Apostolic Tradition* of Saint Hippolytus that the third-century assembly
was the coming together of the whole people of God for the con-
celebration, under the presidency of the clergy, of Christ's saving
deeds. Even the ordination of bishops took place in the assembly with
the consecrating bishop, at the request of all, laying hands on the
bishop-elect, praying while all kept silence, praying in their heart for
the descent of the Spirit.[33]

[25] St. Ignatius of Antioch, "The Letter to the Philadelphians," 7: "Give heed
to the bishop, the priests and the deacons."
[26] St. Ignatius of Antioch, "The Letter to the Ephesians," 4 and 20; and "The
Letter to the Philadelphians," 4.
[27] St. Ignatius of Antioch, "The Letter to the Smyrnaeans," 8; and St. Justin
Martyr, *op. cit.*, 65.
[28] St. Clement of Rome, *op. cit.*, 40.
[29] "The Didache," 15, 1.
[30] St. Clement of Rome, *op. cit.*, 44, 5.
[31] St. Justin Martyr, *op. cit.*, 65.
[32] Tertullian, "Apology," tr. Sister Emily Joseph Daly, D.S.J., in *The Fathers
of the Church*, New York, Fathers of the Church, Inc., 1950, 39.
[33] St. Hippolytus, *The Treatise on the Apostolic Tradition of St. Hippolytus
of Rome*, ed. Rev. Gregory Dix, New York, Macmillan Company, 1937, 2, 4:
"And all shall keep silence praying in their heart for the descent of the Spirit."

Likewise, the meeting for the administration of the sacraments of
initiation is a liturgical celebration of the whole people of God, in
whose midst the neophyte proclaims his faith, while the assembly
responds to his reception of the cup of the eucharist "in the Holy
Spirit in the holy Church" with "Amen." [34] The celebration of the
word of God also takes place in the assembly[35] so their faith will
be established by what they hear;[36] each is to be careful to go to the
assembly where the Holy Spirit abounds[37] and, listening, to respond
by prayers to God's word and Spirit. The love meal (*agape*), too, is
a liturgical gathering with only the baptized present, praying and
singing alleluias together.[38] The ordination rite also implies that the
forgiveness of sins and the loosing of every bond took place in the
holy assembly.[39] The *Didascalia Apostolorum* makes this directly
clear.[40]

Therefore, we may conclude that each gathering of the faithful is
an assembly in the full sense of the word: the holy people of God
called together for the celebration of God's saving deeds in their
midst. Because they are true Christians they gather, and because
they gather they are true Christians. Brought together as the holy
people of God, they are distinguished from the nonbaptized. They
have the right to pray together, to know the secrets of the mysteries,
to assist at the love meal, to choose their leaders, to intervene in the
sacraments of initiation, to participate in all the assemblies, especially
in the eucharist through their common prayers and gifts, and to give
the assent of their amen to the common petitions and offerings; they
have the duty to pray during the day and to live according to the
instructions they have received and responded to, and to live as one

[34] *Ibid.*, 23, 10: "And in ⟨the⟩ Holy Spirit [and] in the Holy Church; and he
shall say: Amen."
[35] *Ibid.*, 33, 2: "And when all have assembled they shall instruct those who are
in the assembly [ἐκκλησία]."
[36] *Ibid.*, 35, 3: ". . . so thy faith will be established by what thou hearest."
[37] *Ibid.*, 35, 3: ". . . let each one be careful . . . to go to the assembly
[ἐκκλησία] to the place where the Holy Spirit abounds."
[38] *Ibid.*, 26, 5: "A catechumen shall not sit at the Lord's Supper"; 26, 31: "Let
all the people answer 'Hallelujah'."
[39] *Ibid.*, 3, 5: "And that by the high priestly Spirit he may have authority 'to
forgive sins' according to Thy Command. . . ."
[40] *Didascalia et Constitutiones Apostolorum*, ed. Francis X. Funk, Paderborn,
Ferdinand Schoenengh, 1905, bk. II, 18, 7: ". . . si is, qui peccavit, paenitentiam
agit ac lacrimatur, recipe eum et tota ecclesia pro eo orante ei manus impone ac
deinde permitte, ut in ecclesia sit. . . ."

of the faithful, for all have the Spirit of God [41] to guide them in the Christian way.

Conclusion

Christ, the same yesterday, today, and forever, is still present in our Christian assemblies, identifying Himself with us. In the celebration of our liturgy, we must be sure not to hide our God; on the contrary, what is of itself invisible and imperceptible to our senses and our intelligence must be made manifest in and through Christ. It is imperative that the liturgical actions within the Christian congregation show and express the divine and eternal reality of the God Who saves us in Christ through His Spirit. In this view of the Church, the participation of the faithful at the liturgical convocations is its central structural and organic element. To be fully effective, the liturgical dialogue must express and reveal on the plane of ritual and symbolic action "the truth of the divine dialogue in which God addresses himself to us, calls us by our name and asks for our faith, our personal and liturgical 'Amen.' " [42] It is evident that this calls for a communication and openness on a higher level than a mere togetherness; it evokes an experience of the mystery of oneness in grace, a presence to one another in Christ, an openness to the reality of the Spirit in and through all who have been brought together in the worshiping assembly.

Thus, in the words of Father Josef Jungmann, it is hoped that the Council provides in the Constitution on the Sacred Liturgy an unexpected confirmation and stimulation of awareness of the Church. For it identifies the Church not as a juridical, authoritative Church of the clergy, nor as an assembly demanded solely by Church law in which the faithful attend a mysterious procedure as spectators, but rather as a gathering which "is itself the true realization of the concept of Church: the visible union of those called by God in Christ." [43]

The more we study the directives of Vatican II, the clearer it becomes that the liturgical action must be a pre-eminent manifestation of the true nature of the Church as well as a true celebration of the

[41] St. Hippolytus, *op. cit.*, 16, 25: "If we have omitted anything, decide ye as is fit; for we all have the Spirit of God."
[42] Fransen, *op. cit.*, p. 191.
[43] Josef Jungmann, S.J., "The Council and Liturgical Reform," in Rahner *et al.*, *op. cit.*, p. 163.

highest mysteries of our faith. A mere hootenanny-togetherness must not be allowed to masquerade as the Christian assembly, in which the light of faith must burn brightly. The liturgy, the Christian community active with Christ in its midst, must express the divine-human dialogue which is its reality.

Our capacity to choose changes constantly with our practice of life.

ERICH FROMM

REVEREND JOHN A. HARDON, S.J.

8   The Challenge of Religious Studies
in State Universities

I doubt if the average Catholic educator is aware of the dramatic changes taking place in the teaching of religion at state universities. He may have heard about the Society for Religion in Higher Education, or have read *The Study of Religion in American Universities* by Robert Michaelsen of the University of California. What he would not be expected to know is that tax-supported colleges and universities are entering the field of religion with a vigor that suggests a change of climate which I consider nothing short of revolutionary.

My own experience at the state university of Western Michigan during the past four years has taught me many things, some of which I would like to share in the hope that the teaching of sacred doctrine may be challenged to improvement and that means may be found for a closer and more effective cooperation between church-related schools and public institutions of higher learning. I have learned that life on a secular campus not only can, but in fact often does bring religion into an urgent focus.

For the sake of convenience, I wish to speak on two levels of the subject: the external challenge of a growing monopoly by state universities, and the internal challenge of academic pluralism that church-related colleges face in competition with secular systems of education. That the two challenges are closely connected and over-lapping is inevitable; yet the concepts they imply are quite distinct, and clarity of distinction here may protect Catholic college administrators from the apologetic tone they sometimes assume in comparing their own schools with secular institutions in the same field.

Why Religious Studies in State Universities?

Community colleges and state universities are entering the field of religion. A recent study by Clyde Holbrook, *Religion, a Humanistic Field*, showed that 45 percent of American state institutions of higher learning have religion departments or chairs,[1] to say nothing of various alternative arrangements for academic work in religion. At the University of Southern Illinois last November, thirty state universities held a consultative conference on the teaching of religion, and I spoke at the conference banquet. Delegates from the ranking schools in the country, the state universities of California and Georgia, of Indiana, Michigan, and Illinois, Texas, Tennessee, and Oklahoma, spent three days discussing religion courses in the regular college curriculum—not whether they were feasible or permissible but how to teach them most effectively. This conference dispelled the last doubt I might have had on whether religion is being taught in tax-supported colleges, and persuaded me that we have seen only the beginning of a new era in the most neglected area of American education.

The question naturally arises, how come? How do you explain the sudden interest in teaching religion on campuses that for generations have been considered forbidden territory? Is it just a passing fad or something deeply rooted in the structure and philosophy of these institutions that brings on this unexpected renascence? Behind the answers to these questions lies the first great challenge to Catholic colleges, which reveals their almost unlimited potentialities for the future.

State universities are beginning to teach religion because they have to. They are growing into a monopoly, and this exposes problems and creates new ones that even twenty years ago were unknown. Religion, they are discovering, is becoming a crucial necessity. Easy access to billions of dollars in tax money has brought them millions of students who cannot afford a church-related college or, if they can, prefer the academic advantages that only money can buy.

But this avalanche of students is precipitating a crisis. Young men and women in college want more than the diluted vocational education to prepare them for a job which until lately has characterized state institutions. Moreover, since state colleges are supported by

[1] Clyde A. Holbrook, *Religion, a Humanistic Field*, Englewood Cliffs, N.J., Prentice-Hall, Inc., 1963.

public funds, they are expected to respond to community needs, and the expectation is becoming more insistent on the part of those who understandably resent their rising monopolization. Finally, the national interest favors a reassessment of a self-imposed neutralism about values and ideals at a time when the country requires nothing so much as intelligent citizens who respect civil authority and whose patriotism has been nourished to love their fellow man even to the point of sacrificing their lives.

Students' Need for a Value-Centered Education

Since 1952 I have been working in the field of religion and public education. My principal involvement has been as a consultant to various associations concerned with training teachers for elementary and secondary public schools. During the past four years, I have taught upward of 1700 students at Western Michigan University.

Out of this fifteen-year experience has come one dominant impression: the young people of America are desperately hungry for religious maturity. They want to learn something more than skills or information, which until now was about all that state universities could offer them. Their deepest need is to make sense of human existence, to learn how to resolve the dilemma of preparing for a career and of becoming themselves. I have recently written a book called *The Hungry Generation*, based exclusively on what my students at Western Michigan have told me about themselves.

These young people want above all (even when they cannot vocalize their needs) to acquire some value centrality in their studies in order to keep from becoming schizophrenic personalities—one half trying to understand money, marriage, sex, and politics, and the other half concerned with the soul-searching questions of life and the mystery of death.

They want direction and purpose to their studies, without which all the classes and courses would be useless. Why exert themselves unless they have a goal in life? Why prod the mind to intellectual effort or train the emotions to self-control? I recall struggling with three attempted suicides among the undergraduates in December of 1965; the experience opened my eyes to the lost dimension in secular higher education.

The students have an intense desire for knowledge of *why* they believe what they do or why anyone should believe at all. Two kinds of students come to a state college: those who enter with a definite religious commitment, and the minority who have only a vague notion of what commitment means.

Every member of either group, however, is looking for the intellectual integrity he has not been able to secure before college.

As psychologists explain it, the whole period from infancy to manhood forms one grand cycle. Its stage of romance stretches across the first dozen years of life, its stage of precision covers the school period of secondary education, and its stage of generalization is the time of entrance into adulthood.

For those whose formal education continues beyond high school, the university or its equivalent is the great period of generalization, the spirit of which should dominate a university, where the mind is developed not merely to think but to think critically and constructively.

What state universities are reluctantly finding, and what Catholic colleges dare not forget, is that no significant area of human experience may be omitted or minimized from such constructive analysis —notably including religious faith.

Part of this process of philosophizing is to challenge existing beliefs, to ask and come to grips with questions like: Is there a God or a life after death? Is faith itself only a projection of the ego—as Feuerbach would have it—or the acceptance on God's word of an objective revelation to man?

The students' readiness to face up to these questions is certain, and it reflects an urgent spiritual need. Yet some Catholic colleges are cutting back their offerings in theology and dropping courses in philosophy, at a time when state universites are creating departments of religion to meet this demand for value centrality in higher education.

Monopoly and American Democracy

Another reason that tax-supported colleges are going into the business of religion arises from the criticism they expect from those who are not happy to see public funds diverted so unilaterally in favor of state universities. They are growing to a point unprecedented in American history. In California 83 percent of college students are in tax-supported institutions, in Michigan 81 percent, and in Wisconsin 75 per cent.

At least three classes of Americans are showing concern over this trend, and any realistic appraisal of religion in state or private universities cannot ignore their concern.

The first are those who fear the state's expanding control of education. With John Stuart Mill, they feel that "A general state education is a mere contrivance for moulding people to be exactly like one another." In a word, they dread the prospect of a nation molded by a government to think what the government wants, without the protection that religion gives from within man's soul against the coercive forces of political expediency.

The second group are those who see private colleges and universities, mostly church-related, dwindling out of existence for lack of funds—now being diverted to tax-supported institutions. They point out, for example, that in Wisconsin the state university and colleges had a recent freshman class increase of 20 percent. All the state's independent colleges, on the other hand, suffered a freshman decrease of 2 percent.

The third class consists of religious bodies and agencies. These people are not looking to state universities to do their work, but believe that if higher education is to train the mind in every form of human knowledge, religion stands by right, and not by sufferance or apology, as an important phenomenon deserving scholarly study and explanation in colleges which this group supports.

At this point, I believe the Catholic Church in America is at the crossroad of its history in higher education. Bishops and major superiors will soon have to make a crucial decision that may affect the Church for the next century or more. The dilemma they face is very simple to express, but not so easy to resolve.

The cold fact is that Catholics are going to secular, mostly state universities in increasing numbers—almost a million this academic year, compared with less than four hundred thousand in all Catholic colleges and universities combined. Anyone familiar with secular education knows that the faith and moral standards of many students suffer traumatic shock when exposed to it. Personally, I am inclined to think that, in the majority of cases, religious values are seriously impaired.

Strong voices are being heard suggesting that the Church shift its emphasis from Catholic colleges to the secular campus, that manpower be directed toward the newly founded departments of religion at state universities, and that if necessary Catholic institutions close in favor of full-scale involvement in state-controlled universities.

At the other extreme are some who feel that nothing should be done. If most Catholics go to secular schools, so be it. Those who prefer (and can afford) a church-affiliated college will be accommodated, even if they are a shrinking minority. Already we hear talk about the "small remnant" who remain faithful to the Gospel, and the need for reconciling oneself to the inevitable.

I suppose there are not many complete absorptionists (the first type) or isolationists (second type). Yet I sense that a general feeling of defeatism pervades the atmosphere, and that more would settle for the status quo than face the future with the courage and hope which these changing times demand.

The Welfare of the Nation

The final explanation for the sudden increase of religious studies in state university curricula stems from a fear that somehow the welfare of American society is at stake.

The issue is not complicated: if the principles on which our culture is founded are those of Judeo-Christianity, and if these principles are to remain vital in the lives of our people, can the universities which educate most of America's leaders ignore their responsibility to a society which makes their very existence possible?

Christian educators who are not Catholic have been the prime movers in giving religion its rightful position in the university curriculum. Dr. George W. Forell, Dean of the School of Religion at the State University of Iowa, speaks for thousands of public educators:

> The scientific investigation of religious faith and its various expressions is one of the oldest academic enterprises. For many centuries, since their inception, universities have been the centers of theological learning. The Sorbonne, the University of Vienna, Oxford and Cambridge, Heidelberg and Wittenberg were publicly supported universities whose reputation was largely derived from first-rate courses of instruction in religion. When Shakespeare had Hamlet go somewhat unhistorically to the University of Wittenberg (founded in the sixteenth century), it was because the great English dramatist was familiar with the fame of its theological faculty.
>
> To deny a university the right to deal in a scholarly and scientific manner with religion is to deny it the right to be a complete university. This means that any American university, regardless of its source of support, should have a faculty which could deal competently and sympathetically with the phenomenon of religion in general and the Western heritage, dominated by the Judaeo-Christian tradition, in

particular. In other cultures the emphasis might be appropriately different.[2]

Other spokesmen for the state university claim, with Harvey Cox, that we have seen the last of elite education. The kind of society we shall live in during the next twenty years will make a college diploma as important as a high school diploma was to our fathers.

A cybernetic culture requires a larger percentage of educated and technically adept people. Making it possible for all qualified young people to go to college is not just a handout by the welfare state. It is a grave necessity. Ignoramuses cannot manage an automated society.

These are the salient facts about the *body* of a university as it faces the future, its statistical development in numbers, equipment, and size of budget. But what about its *soul?*

For years a variety of factors has conspired to produce a cleavage between the sacred and secular, between God and man. One result has been the tragic bifurcation between theology and humanism, of which the very term *secular university* is a revealing symptom.

But society, like the individuals composing it, cannot subsist for long on this double standard. It needs, as do individuals, a sense of unity in its thinking, to be communicated by potentially the most unitive force in America, the university—provided the university offers a basis of unification in teaching the science of God.

The Challenge to American Catholicism

These developments challenge American Catholics across the spectrum of their educational thinking: to improve the departments of religion in their own institutions, at any cost and even at the sacrifice of other segments of the curriculum; to assist secular colleges in their laudable effort to introduce and upgrade the teaching of religion on the secular campus; and all the while to work toward greater equity in the distribution of tax money, which now creates a terrible imbalance weighing against private colleges and universities.

Improving theology courses in Catholic colleges goes together with offering assistance to secular institutions. It would be a grave

[2] The complete text of Dr. Forell's statement on religion in state universities may be obtained by writing to him at the State University of Iowa, Iowa City.

mistake to weaken existing church-related schools in order to staff
incipient religion departments in public-supported universities. Competition is keen enough without our adding to the problem by skim-
ming off the best talent among the teachers. Moreover, it is a mirage
to suppose that Catholic educators (especially priests and religious)
would enjoy the kind of freedom they now have at schools under
the Church's auspices. They can be hired, and urged to join the faculty of a state university, but the price they may have to pay will be
adaptation to the norms of an institution whose main concerns are
pragmatic and not religious. The priest on a secular faculty is treated
more as a symbol than as a scholar; he is generally not seriously encouraged to exploit the resources of faith in the widest interest of his
students.

Training competent laymen for teaching positions in secular colleges is years overdue. What is needed is a steady supply of well-
chosen and highly trained instructors who have academic degrees
(which means doctorates) in theology, the biblical sciences, and
Church history. With few exceptions, Catholic universities still fear
to give laymen advanced degrees in the sacred sciences. Seminaries
are even more intransigent. Catholic divinity schools might learn
from the example of Protestant seminaries, some of which are currently training more educators for college departments of religion
than clergymen for the ministry. A drastic revision along these lines
would be in full accord with the spirit of the Second Vatican Council. Lay professors are in special demand, since most secular colleges
prefer laymen to clerics, whose very presence is a constant reminder
of "sectarianism" on a nonsectarian campus.

The heart of the problem remains, however; and those who are
most familiar with the scene wonder whether Catholics have not been
too slow in appealing to the sense of equity of their fellow Americans for a just share in the tax money which presently goes exclusively to public universities.

Freedom and justice for all persons, whatever their religious beliefs, is a basic principle of American democracy. The ultimate
practical application of this principle is that the state or federal government or both should provide educational benefits by way of
voucher for all young people, and not only for those attending tax-
supported schools.

It is a violation of both freedom and justice that a university student who resides in a state must attend a tax-supported college in

that state if he is to receive the benefits which the state has decreed to give university students.

Justice is violated because every college graduate is expected to repay society for his education by becoming a productive citizen. Yet unless he has attended a tax-supported institution, he has not received his educational benefits. Freedom is violated because if the person desiring an education must attend an institution designated by the state, whatever its philosophy, he is being forced to conform with that institution's principles of operation.

We boast that in the United Sates we have and foster a pluralistic society. On a college level this should mean that a variety of institutions with a variety of religious philosophies can exist and continue to prosper. It should mean that citizens of America have the economic freedom to attend that college which most agrees with their own religious outlook on life. Yet the facts belie the claim. When the best talent at a Catholic university is enticed elsewhere in one year—some by the mere expedient of a doubling of their salaries—it is naive to talk about free enterprise.

One passage in the Vatican Council's decree on education is directly relevant. It spells out in detail the state's rights and duties, with special attention to a religious pluralism which deserves more study than we have so far given it:

> . . . it is incumbent upon the state to provide all citizens with the opportunity to acquire an appropriate degree of cultural enrichment, and with the proper preparation for exercising their civic rights and duties. Therefore, the state itself ought to protect the right of children to receive an adequate schooling. . . .
> But it must keep in mind the principle of subsidiarity, so that no kind of school monopoly arises. For such a monopoly would militate against the native rights of the human person, the development and spread of culture, the peaceful association of citizens, and the pluralism which exists today in very many societies.[3]

At the risk of being misunderstood, I submit that the best long-range solution for the religious development of Catholics on secular campuses is not to rush into their departments of religion. These may be helped in every way possible, notably through the provision of competent lay personnel trained in Catholic graduate schools of theology. But all the while the deeper issue must be kept in mind.

Catholics have a duty as citizens to see to it that our society main-

---

[3] Declaration on Christian Education, sec. 6.

tains an atmosphere where religious pluralism can flourish, and where every citizen (Christian, Jew, or otherwise) can receive a college education in a school that most nearly corresponds with his own philosophy of life.

Pluralism in a Catholic University

Besides the external challenge to its very existence created by a rampant state education, which is now competing with the Catholic college in teaching religion, there is a more subtle internal challenge to it from the question of pluralism.

Secular universities pose as protectors of the freedom of the human spirit and of the liberty of divergent faiths. By contrast, church-related schools are labeled *sectarian* because they ostensibly seek to advance the cause of their own religionists with no regard for the faith (or unbelief) of those outside the pale.

Let me say at the outset that one kind of pluralistic attitude is intolerable on a Catholic campus: the agnosticism of a teacher who ridicules the faith of his students on the premise that no one knows the truth and that all religious belief is pure subjectivism.

But a pluralism which respects the faith of others, studies different religious systems, and wrestles with alien modes of thought not only belongs in Catholic colleges but, in the present age of dialogue, is an academic requisite.

On the broadest scale in American colleges is Christian pluralism, with over two hundred denominations stemming from the Protestant Reformation. Time and again students have told me that one of the principal benefits they have gained from attending a state university is a knowledge and appreciation of Protestantism through courses in comparative American religion.

For Catholic educators responsive to the openness of the ecumenical movement, this should be a powerful incentive to teach and study Christianity across the whole gamut of its manifestations outside the stream of Catholicism. In fact, the greatest hope of the ecumenical movement lies in the colleges and seminaries under the aegis of the Church.

Catholic higher education should be adjusted to the ecumenical times, above all by instilling in the Church's leaders a desire to share the knowledge of Christ with all Christians, not only with professed Catholics.

The whole college curriculum, and not alone in theology, should gradually be adapted to meet the new needs. In the words of the Council, "We must get to know the outlook of our separated brethren. To achieve this purpose, study is of necessity required, and this must be pursued with a sense of realism and good will. Catholics, who already have a proper grounding, need to acquire a more adequate understanding of the respective doctrines of our separated brethren, their history, their spiritual and liturgical life, their religious psychology and cultural background." [4] This mandate pertains to all Catholics, laymen as well as religious and priests.

I like the expression "with a sense of realism and good will," describing how the study of other Christian traditions should be made. Realism means I do not ignore or underestimate the differences that divide Catholicism from other systems of Christian thought. Realism protects undergraduates from falling prey to that simplistic irenicism which seeks to reduce the Council of Trent to outdated formulas, and sees in the Roman primacy an obstacle to its own concept of Christian unity. At the same time, good will preserves students from looking for defects in those who are not Catholic, instead of finding what they have in common on which to build an edifice of spirituality.

Equally urgent, for the sake of Christian pluralism, is the introduction in Catholic colleges and universities of courses on world religion, which state institutions have been teaching for years. As far as I know, every tax-supported college in the country offers some form of study of the world's living faiths. On the other hand, with a few rare exceptions Catholic institutions of higher learning ignore the religious beliefs of more than half the human race as though they did not exist. No wonder they are accused of sectarianism and charged with perpetuating the closed mind.

Fifty years ago it would have been premature to speak of a dialogue with the great religions of the East. But much has happened since the turn of the century to change the refrain that East is East and West is West and never the twain shall meet. For the first time in their history, the Oriental religions have made available to Western readers the full riches of their sacred writings. Since modern science has brought the two extremes into easy contact, almost erasing the geographic distances between nations, ideas are being carried

---

[4] See Decree on Ecumenism, sec. 9.

from one end of the world to the other with the swiftness of thought.

We have scarcely recovered from one conflict in the East and are on the verge of precipitating another and worse conflagration. Yet ironically we know next to nothing about the religious culture of the Orient. A millennium of missionary effort has brought Christ only to a fraction of the Asian people; but how could we expect them to be interested in our religion if we never bothered even to learn the spelling of Buddha's name or cared to know that Hindus have scriptures which antedate the New Testament by two thousand years?

Teaching comparative religion will soon become mandatory. I am currently working as consultant with the state board of education of Florida, helping plan courses on the major living faiths for the secondary public schools of the state. At a two-day conference in Tallahassee in the spring of 1966, I was inspired to see the progress which secular educators are making to implement the program by the fall of 1967. Not satisfied with a full-blown curriculum on the university level, the high schools supported by public funds are doing the same. As I conferred with the Florida committee, I could not avoid thinking what a long way Catholic schools have to go before they shed the stereotype which identifies their philosophy as denominational because it ventures so seldom outside the precincts of Catholic Christianity.

I have saved the most difficult kind of pluralism for last. Other religions than the Catholic are, after all, believers in some form of deity, and even Buddhism is basically theistic, despite its reputation to the contrary. But a university lives up to its stature when it faces systems of thought that are alien and antithetical to the professed beliefs of the students.

Let me make myself clear. A Catholic college has the right to determine its own philosophy of education and not be censured for insisting on academic freedom for the institution. If only individual freedom as against institutional were defended, no organized body in the country could long remain safe, and we would soon see the end of any society that individuals decided was foreign to their taste.

This is not to say, however, that no writer or system hostile to the established creed should be taught. The roster of names that come to mind is endless, and the challenges these people offer to Catholic students are vital, with the vitality that secular schools claim to possess and that church-related institutions notoriously lack. Freud and

James in psychology; Pierce, Dewey, and Whitehead in philosophy; Marx and Engels in political science; Durkheim and Meade in sociology; Coulton, Gibbon, and the Beards in history; Harnack, Feuerbach, Hegel, and Renan in religion; Altizer, Hamilton, and Robinson in theology—these are only samples of the exposure that any viable education ought to provide for mature men and women in college.

Until teachers are prepared to handle orthodoxy and heterodoxy, and are willing to trust themselves and the faith they profess to contradiction from the best intellectual critics of Catholicism and Christianity, they are open to invidious comparison with secular (especially state) university educators whose main boast is that they are free to examine what Catholic institutions dare not touch.

The hallmark of an educated man these days is that his mind has not been confined to seeing only one religion or one philosophy, or only what supports his own convictions. By this standard, Catholic colleges are challenged by a prosperous tax-supported system of education to reassess their approach to human and divine knowledge. They have nothing to lose and everything to gain by rising to the demands of this challenge.

The moral structure of Marx's myth is related to that of Hegel's philosophical religion of self. . . .

ROBERT C. TUCKER

VERY REVEREND ANTHONY SCHILLACI, O.P.

9   Modern Man's Morality Play

In Federico Fellini's *La Dolce Vita*, we find one of the most striking images of the Church's involvement with the cinema created in recent times. A helicopter is carrying a giant statue of Christ along the life-giving aqueducts leading to Rome. The aqueducts are in ruins, but a new source of vitality and a contemporary means of communication are once more bringing Christ to the center of the Church.

As the Church today, swept by the revolution of Vatican II, seeks "to unfold more fully . . . to the whole world its own inner nature and universal mission" (Constitution on the Church, sec. 1), it is essential that we not dissociate that revolution from a parallel upheaval in cultural communications. I am speaking of the transition from a literary to a visual culture in the United States and Europe. Unlike political revolutions, those which take place in communications do not display their violent and radical nature to the casual observer. We hear a few rumblings, such as the reluctance of some Catholics to diminish their dependence on the missal, and this is one of the few hints that the written word has been displaced, thrown out of its centuries-old place of superiority by a quiet coup of the visual image. Beneath these surface signs lies the submerged, hidden mass of a vast and complex change which some have likened to that in ancient Greece, when the culture of a nation was first committed to writing.

The visual age is a gift to man by electric technology, the direct successor to the technology of print and mass production. Eventually we will see the temple of the written word, the library, torn down and replaced by instant data-recovery systems that will signal the replacement of the printing press by the computer. Of course, we

93

will resist until the pressures become unbearable. We are resisting
the visual age today with a kind of futile frenzy that escapes or denies
reality outright. The average young person today sees twenty films
for every book he reads, and yet we continue to structure our curriculum as if the printing press had just been invented. Occasionally
the holes in our logic will appear, and the dropout problem is one
of these. But do we recognize it as a sign that the school exclusively
oriented to the written word can no longer hold a visually oriented
generation, which has been conditioned to respond to the image?

The Church cannot afford so to concentrate upon her own revolution that she is blinded to a larger revolution in the context of which
it is taking place. In an age of rapid change, religion has no corner
on irrelevancy. Depending on how quickly and accurately we receive
the message, however, we will develop attitudes that commit us
either hopefully to the future or hopelessly to the past. If *aggiornamento* is an invitation to live in this age as part of this age, then it is
an invitation to the Christian to come alive in a visual age. The most
complete visual statement of our day is found in the art of the film,
modern man's morality play.

The posture of fear and suspicion, which has been the Church's
response to the mass media until now, must give way to one of acceptance and witness before we can enter into any fruitful collaboration with the means of communication. In $8\frac{1}{2}$, the experience of the
film director in his interview with the Cardinal shows the suffocating
irrelevancy that results when the Church tells the artist not to touch
on the deepest religious and philosophical themes. We can sympa-
thize with Guido in that scene as he lapses into a delightful recollec-
tion of Saraghina, dancing the rumba for her young clientele. For
the Church to refuse these means of communication would be as un-
thinkable as refusing to use the Roman roads in the time of Paul or
to print the Bible in the time of Gutenberg. However, to accept the
media is to accept responsibility for a new incarnation of the Gospel
in the unique idiom of each mode of communication.

This is a serious responsibility, and one which is not faced by any
superficial acceptance of the latest communications techniques. A
common first reaction is to take the cinema, for example, as a gim-
mick, a way to "reach" people, to get them into the church basement,
to hold them still while we administer the same anesthetic. Such
updating, like a new coat of paint, soon peels off, leaving the surface
unchanged. A more common error is to look upon the film medium

as an ideal way to transmit the traditional message in the traditional style. The television preacher who stands frozen before the camera, shouting and gesticulating as if his audience were a hundred yards away, is an example of this error. But there is a far more subtle error, based as these are upon a failure to realize, as Marshall McLuhan has made so clear, that "The medium is the message."

The mass media communicate much more by what they are than by what they say. The social and psychic powers of film and television are only indirectly related to what these media present on their screens. Their force as instruments of social change, for example, is more directly dependent upon the modes of sense perception they create than upon the ideas they convey. This assertion is not merely an updated version of the dictum "It's not what you say but how you say it." In most communication, how you say it *is* what you say. The preacher who presents the Gospel in a lifeless, listless manner is preaching disbelief, and very effectively.

There is much more at stake here than the form and content dichotomy. To conceive of the media as new, convenient ways of transmitting the old message is what McLuhan calls "technological idiocy," a part of "the current somnambulism" of the unaware. No medium of communication is neutral, a kind of impartial pipeline through which various materials can be pumped. Not only does the medium shape the message, but in terms of sheer effect, it is what is communicated. This fact is difficult to perceive because each medium takes the previous medium as its content, thereby giving the illusion of a perfect continuity. The novel becomes the content of the film, and the film becomes the content of the television program. Nevertheless, it is a changed content, for the medium has entered into it and changed it radically. The import of print is not so much what is read but the fact that men will look to the book instead of the spoken word for knowledge and experience. The import of a visual age is that men now look to the image, and not primarily to the book, for meaning.

Can the Church submit the Gospel to such a transformation, in which the medium is likely to transform the content? This is a question which stands before any wholehearted attempt to collaborate with the media in our day. Is it not the duty of the Church to preserve the content of revelation intact? The question betrays the mentality that is at the base of most objections to using the media. It is not a content but a Person whom we preach and teach, and unless this Person speaks in the language of the age, we have betrayed our apostolic mission. The risk that we face today is the same one taken when the first painter decided to portray Christ in the catacombs, or when the stained glass windows of Chartres were commissioned, or when the Bible was printed, or when any new means was used to present the Gospel. Each age must experience a new incarnation of the Gospel, one that communicates with the age in its own terms. It is the artist who frequently provides the language for such communication.

Cinema as the Art of the Age

If we turn to a single art to learn this visual language, the film presents itself as the art that speaks for our age. It is, for one thing, the art most alive today. Far from having been academicized into the irrelevancy of "culture," the film is still searching out the possibilities of its medium under the pioneering efforts of Bergman and Fellini, Bresson and Kurasawa, Richardson and Antonioni. We are in fact in the midst of a renaissance of film art which is as much signaled by *Thunderball* as by *Juliet of the Spirits*. If we shake off a limiting perspective of years, we will realize that Shakespeare's time saw just such an exuberance of dramatic activity, with much of it destined for oblivion but a substantial core that was sure to endure.

Television is a more contemporary visual medium than film, but it has neither the control nor the fullness of concept that are necessary for art. The film is the complete visual statement, one that evokes a response from the generation cued to the image. It is this rapport with an age that has placed upon the cinema the role of modern man's morality play.

Cinema as Morality Play

The morality play of the Middle Ages was a spontaneous growth of religious drama designed to edify as it entertained. While we are inclined to look upon its development as a decline into mere entertainment, we should recall that it only retained its power to edify as long as it remained entertainment. If this is true, then we should not be surprised to learn that the cinema became a morality play by way of entertainment which underwent a certain evolution we may describe as the stages of mirror, myth, and then morality.

The film is a mirror of reality because it reflects reality in a way that no other art form can reflect it. Novels, poems, and paintings hold a mirror to reality in a sense, but their images reflect an artist's conception of reality. The cinema presents an "image" which witnesses the real existence, at one time, of what is shown, for the object itself creates the photographic impression by its own light. This testimony gives the documentary film its great authority, and makes every film in a sense "realistic." Through its ability to capture motion, to manipulate time and space as dimensions of motion, the film captivates the audience by a continuing act of recognition and participation.

We might mention in this context how perfectly the cinema reflects reality today, that is, the world view of contemporary man. This new world view is that of a cosmic whole in which mass and energy are convertible, in which all motion is resolved into a space-time continuum. The motion picture is bound to the new way of thought and life in which time and movement, energy and dynamics arc considered more representative of reality than matter conceived as a stable solid in a stable cosmos. The film is also instrumentally a machine art for a technological age. Its surrealist eye devours space by its omnipresence, reflecting the relativity of Einstein's privileged observer on another planet, under whose surveillance all processes are reversed and transformed. The dominance of motion, held captive on a strip of celluloid, enables the cinema to establish a sweeping relativity of time, telescoping and expanding it, revising our entire notion of sequence and simultaneity. More important than these similarities, the film gives us an evolutionary universe, a functional view of nature rather than static essences, a continuity between all living and nonliving processes, rather than a rigid system of classes.

Perfect as its reflection of reality may be, it is not adequate for film art merely to record reality, unless we intend a documentary work. The film must so organize its materials, reshaping reality by manipulating time and space, altering the tempo and rhythm of life, that realities speak not of themselves alone but of all mankind. Out of the same need that caused Babylonian and Greek to forge a mythical explanation of their universe, the cinema takes its complex tool and orders its beautiful reflections of reality into a coherent world view with man at its center. The contemporary film, then, is myth as well as mirror. Sometimes the mythical structure is more apparent, as in *Sundays and Cybele*. Many other films either take an expressly allegorical form or at least highly organize their materials around certain ideas. We need only mention *Macario, The Given Word, Ikiru*, and

Juliet of the Spirits to indicate this myth-making quality of the cinema. Of course, we do not mention the commercial myth propagated by Hollywood, because such has little if anything to do with reality in the first place.

If we were to look into the aesthetics of film for the reasons it can order reality into a mythical whole, we would decide upon the editing process. This essential creative activity of filmmaking is the joining together of thousands of images to create a motion picture that has continuity and unity. Since the film lacks a material that is consumed or radically altered in use, it greatly resembles music, especially in the editing process. The images are not reshaped but joined one to the other according to temporal and spatial ratios which are determined by their associations with one another.

Editing gives its images not a sequential order of cause and effect but a consequential order that furnishes new meaning to the images themselves. The addition of one shot to another is not a quantitatively but a qualitatively distinct entity. One image is used to interpret another; for example, an audience who sees a bowl of soup and a man's face will immediately conclude that he is hungry. This association of images is the basis for the cinematic myth. It is also the reason films concentrate so heavily on psychological dramas which explore the unconscious or subconscious states of its characters. The motion picture resembles our very thought processes, which it can re-create on the screen in such films as *The Trial*, all of whose characters are part of one psyche; $8\frac{1}{2}$, where the past is shown to be lived in every moment of the present; or *Loneliness of the Long-Distance Runner*, in which the central character determines his identity out of the assembled fragments of his psychological states. The variety of associations available to film art is practically infinite, and their complexity has not begun to be exhausted. The possibilities for myth, then, are unlimited.

Is there need for anything more than mirror and myth? Yes. The one element missing from this process by which film records reality and organizes it into coherent unities is the orientation that makes these wholes significant for man. The ancient morality plays amuse us today with their naive portrayals of good and evil, God and the devil. Nevertheless, they express a human desire to discover in art a way of life. The stage has for a long time lectured the audience from the casebooks of Sigmund Freud, and more recently from the writings of the existentialist poet-philosophers. Although these examples seem to moralize rather than delight, they nonetheless point toward the possibility of communicating moral truth by beauty without descending to propaganda. The enduring films have been morality plays in this sense of the word, for they have succeeded in telling man truths about himself, about his relations with God and men, that cannot help but alter his life.

The power of cinema as morality play is based upon an ontological reason, one allied to the very role of man as creator. What constitutes creativity in man is his ability to establish new relationships between existing realities. The association of images in the film is only one of many ways in which an artist unites distinct realities by an analogy. The artist produces forms which actually exist within the analogy of being and furthermore constitute a new entity by contributing to our understanding of being through that analogy. Of the many human activities which terminate in the concrete singular and are yet not considered creative (generation, manufacturing, and the like), art is conceived as creative because its supersensual, superconcrete, and supersingular product succeeds through the artistic imagination in being a unique existent, and at the same time like every other in the universe; a universal idea and a sensible detail; a symbol of all and yet so perfectly possessive of its own identity that it exists as one.

In regard to the unique idiom of film art, we can trace its role as morality play to the insight it gives us into the human condition, particularly through the use of the closeup. The power of the human face to express the spiritual nature of man is incalculable. No one who has assimilated the extreme closeup of Cabiria's companion when it becomes clear that he intends to kill her can remain indifferent to the human capacity for evil. And again in *Nights of Cabiria*, no one who sees Giulietta Masina smile into the camera at the ending can doubt the indestructibility of the human spirit or the regenerative power of love. We have largely lost the wonder and amazement of early audiences receiving their first exposure to the power of the human face upon the screen after D. W. Griffith invented the closeup. We can experience that power in the countenance of Patricia Gozzi in *Sundays and Cybele*, or in Madeleine's face, a mask of grief at the end of the story.

The film is modern man's morality play because it tells him how to be more human. In focusing upon the problems of modern man, the cinema portrays individuals who stand for all of us, suffering the agony of their humanity and its joy. The problems themselves read like a catalogue of human concern: the alienation of man in Antonioni; the craving for love in Fellini; the communal nature of truth in Kurasawa; the search for God and the battle between good and evil in Bergman. The list is indefinite, but the object of concern is singular—man, in his weakness and nobility, his strength and his failures. Surely, not every theological topic is represented or even hinted at upon the screen, but the focus on man is a concentration upon the object of all revelation, of all divine love, of salvation itself.

Karl Rahner recently in Chicago defined man as the creature open to God, and said that the transcendental theology of the future will be, in effect, a Christian anthropology. There is in this remark a whole theology of the cinema, based upon its unique control over human actions and the human countenance. The teacher of sacred doctrine can no longer afford to ignore the image in a visual age. Intent as we are upon the revolution of Vatican II, we must see it as part of a communications revolution which is producing a new kind of human being. The response to the visual image, which is one of the key elements in the makeup of the new man, must serve as the bridge, the analogy between the Gospel and the world. The film artist is providing us with the language, a superb preconceptual tool for communicating with man on the level of full participation and commitment. We must learn from him how to speak the Gospel with the accents, the syntax, the universality, and the impact of this language. In this way alone can we be open to a collaboration in the universal project of making man more human, so that he can become divine.

Contributors

Katharine T. Hargrove, R.S.C.J., is associate professor of religion at Manhattanville College of the Sacred Heart in Purchase, New York. This year she is on leave of absence at Maryville College in Saint Louis, where she is structuring a course in religion entitled "God and the Film" for upperclassmen, a project she hopes to continue after her return to Manhattanville. In connection with the course, she is gathering material for a book on film education; her edited work *The Star and the Cross* (Bruce Publishing Company, 1966) is being widely used in the implementation of the Second Vatican Ecumenical Council's statement on the Jews, especially in living-room dialogues. Her activities in furthering Judeo-Christian accord won her the Edith Stein Award for 1966. Mother Hargrove's articles, poems, and book reviews have appeared in magazines like *Catholic Mind, Catholic World, America, Religious Education, Interracial Review*, and *Theological Studies*.

Doctor Philip Scharper, executive editor at Sheed & Ward, is well known for his lectures, radio and television appearances, and writings. Recipient of the 1961 Francis Xavier Medal of Xavier University in Cincinnati, Ohio, he served as president of the Religious Education Association of the United States and Canada from 1963 to 1966. In 1964 he was invited to Rome as a consultant for Vatican II's committee established to formulate schema 13, "The Church in the Modern World." Active in the lay apostolate, he contributed to *The Church and the Nations* (Sheed & Ward) and to *The Layman and the Church* (Herder and Herder). In 1959 he edited *American Catholics: A Protestant-Jewish View* (Sheed & Ward). His latest editorial work, *Torah and Gospel: Jewish and Catholic*

102 CONTRIBUTORS

Theology in Dialogue (Sheed & Ward, 1966), has already become something of a classic in living-room dialogue.

Brother C. R. Wilson, F.S.C., is the pen name used by Brother Paul, whose present position is that of resident counselor at De La Salle College in Washington, D.C. His articles in *Review for Religious* and in the *American Ecclesiastical Review* bear the imprint of the modern Christian humanist who deservedly holds a doctorate in psychology. Brother Paul maintains contact with his alma mater by returning each summer to Catholic University to conduct courses in the Pastoral Psychology Institute. He is also a summer faculty member at Georgetown University, where he is a lecturer in the Psychology Department.

Brother C. Stephen Sullivan, F.S.C., is academic vice president at Manhattan College in Riverdale, New York. In addition to a master's degree in classics and another in philosophy, he holds an S.T.L. and an S.T.D. in theology. A member of the Catholic Theological Association, the Catholic Biblical Association, and Phi Beta Kappa, he is treasurer of the Society of Catholic College Teachers of Sacred Doctrine. As author and editor, his works are *Formulation of Tridentine Doctrine on Merit,* which appeared in 1959, and *Readings in Sacramental Theology,* published in 1963.

Reverend Joseph A. Travers, O.S.F.S., is presently assistant professor of theology at La Salle College in Philadelphia, Pennsylvania. His work in the past includes six years in the missions at Namaqualand in South Africa, a fruitful period that brought him new insights for his teaching career in this country, especially for his courses conducted at Blessed Sacrament College, Cornwells Heights, Torresdale, Pennsylvania. His article on "Religious Life" has recently appeared in *Salesian Studies* and is a vital witness from one who is director of Pastoral Theology in the Eastern Province of the Oblates of St. Francis de Sales.

Reverend John J. Powell, S.J., is a member of the Bellarmine School of Theology in North Aurora, Illinois. Recently he was elected chairman for the Chicago region of the Society of Catholic College Teachers of Sacred Doctrine, for which he wrote "The Catholic College Student and His Struggle with Faith." In 1958 his book *A Stranger at Your Door* was published by the Bruce Publishing Company. This theology of the Church preluded the 1960 appearance of his doctoral dissertation for the Gregorian Institute in Rome entitled *A Theology of the Apostolate of the Church*. In process at present is his work *The Church as a Supernatural Mystery*, part of a series of college theology texts being published by Bruce. As evidenced in the stimulating booklet which he edited, *The Retreat Master Faces the Nun in the Modern World*, Father Powell is very active not only as theologian and author but as retreat master.

Sister Roderick O'Neil, R.S.H.M., is currently chairman of the Religion Department at Marymount College in Tarrytown, New York. While pursuing her studies at Fordham University and at Union Theological Seminary, Sister still finds time to review books, to contribute to texts like *The Social Doctrine of the Church*, and to gain "value experience" of her favorite idea of "encompassing" by taking part in a sociocultural program conducted in a depressed area near Tarrytown in the summer of 1965.

Sister Mary Anthony Wagner, O.S.B., is a professor in the Theology Department of the College of St. Benedict and a regular member of the faculty of the Graduate School in Sacred Studies at St. John's University, Collegeville, Minnesota. Sister's articles have appeared in *Sponsa Regis*, *The Living Parish*, *The Catholic Educator*, *Journal of Religious Instruction*, *The American Benedictine Review*, and *Benet*. Greatly in demand as a speaker, Sister Mary Anthony has spoken to audiences at the American National Liturgical Week in 1958 and 1963; to members of the Society of Catholic College Teachers of Sacred Doctrine gathered for their national meeting in 1963, she presented her ideas on "Christian Life in the Mystery of the Church." In a workshop conducted with Father Herman Schmidt, S.J., in Fargo, North Dakota, during the summer of 1965, she discussed "The Renewal of the Liturgy in the Convent."

Reverend John A. Hardon, S.J., formerly associate professor of comparative religion at Western Michigan University, is presently visiting professor there as well as associate professor of systematic theology at the Bellarmine School of Theology in North Aurora, Illinois. He has written about a hundred articles for periodicals here and in Europe dealing with religious history and with current problems arising from the pluralistic society in America. His books include *The Protestant Churches in America* (1956), now in its third edition and eighth printing, and a 1959 Spanish edition, *Las Iglesias protestantes de America; All My Liberty* (1959); *Christianity in Conflict* (1959), a sequel to the earlier volume on Protestantism; *For Jesuits*, edited (1963); *Teaching the Devotion to the Sacred Heart*, coauthored with Thomas Diehl (1963); and *Religions of the World* (1963), now in its second edition and fourth printing, which also has a 1965 German edition published at Zurich.

Very Reverend Anthony Schillaci, O.P., is professor of metaphysics and subprior at Aquinas Institute in River Forest, Illinois. Given his rich background in literature, philosophy, and theology, Father Schillaci justly named one of his works *The Starting Point of Metaphysics*. Having already had his "New Cinema for a New Society" published in *Drama Critique* and his "Religion and Cinema: A Cultural Exorcism" in *Catholic Mind*, he is looking forward to the appearance of "Modern Man's Morality Play" in *New City*, "Bergman's Vision of Good and Evil" in *Listening*, and "Use of Films in Religious Preaching and Teaching" in *Cross and Crown*. Father Schillaci hopes to expand the article in *Cross and Crown* into a book, a practical outcome of his approach to implementing his ideas by conducting film workshops.

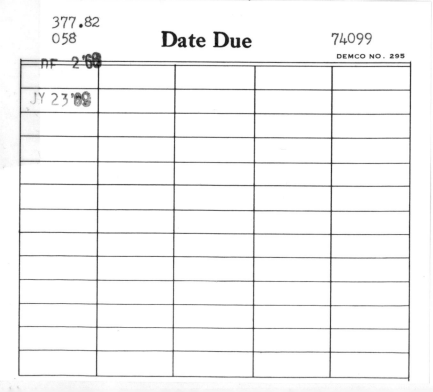